Reimagining African Scholarship:

A Convivial Approach Beyond the Single Story

Francis B. Nyamnjoh

Langaa Research & Publishing CIG
Mankon, Bamenda

Publisher:
Langaa RPCIG
Langaa Research & Publishing Common Initiative Group
P.O. Box 902 Mankon
Bamenda
North West Region
Cameroon
Langaagrp@gmail.com
www.langaa-rpcig.net

Distributed in and outside N. America by
African Books Collective
orders@africanbookscollective.com
www.africanbookscollective.com

ISBN-10: 9956-0-0362-X

ISBN-13: 978-9956-0-0362-4

Table of Contents

Introduction

This book is a timely and comprehensive exploration of the multifaceted challenges and transformative possibilities within African scholarship and publishing. It brings together three scholarly essays that critically analyse the historical and contemporary forces shaping knowledge production about and within the African continent, ultimately advocating for a reimagined approach that prioritises inclusivity, collaboration, and decolonisation.

The collection is structured around three core themes, each representing a crucial dimension of the ongoing conversation about the future of African scholarship.

Part I: Reimagining African Scholarship: Politics of Knowledge and the Call for Conviviality

The book opens by interrogating the very foundations of knowledge production in the context of Africa. It argues that African scholarship must explicitly acknowledge the global power dynamics that influence what knowledge is produced, validated, and consumed. This essay challenges the persistent "outward gaze" that has often characterised African scholarly writing, wherein scholars feel compelled to conform to Eurocentric expectations in terms of methodology, publication venues, and even the very questions deemed worthy of inquiry.

The essay calls for a decisive break from this pattern, emphasising the need for African scholars to critically re-evaluate the tendency to devalue local knowledge, languages, and perspectives in favour of external validation. Decolonisation, it is asserted, is not merely a political aspiration but an intellectual imperative that demands a fundamental shift in how African scholars perceive and engage with their own contexts.

A key concept introduced in this essay is that of "convivial scholarship." This paradigm shift proposes a move away from rigid, exclusionary models of academic inquiry towards a more fluid, collaborative, and inclusive approach. Convivial scholarship recognises the inherent incompleteness of all knowledge systems and the importance of embracing mobility, exchange, and interconnectedness. It champions the idea that knowledge is not a static entity but rather an ongoing process of becoming, shaped by encounters, dialogue, and diverse perspectives.

The essay also critically examines the role of scholarly writing itself, moving beyond a narrow focus on technical proficiency to emphasise the importance of clear argumentation, contextual awareness, and reflexivity. It addresses the challenges faced by African scholars navigating a competitive global publishing landscape and calls for a more nuanced understanding of the relationship between content, technique, message, and messenger.

Part II: Embracing Incompleteness: Metaphors, Mobility, and the Dynamics of Knowledge Exchange

Building on the theoretical framework established in the first essay, the book delves deeper into the practical implications of convivial scholarship. It employs rich metaphors and storytelling, drawing on African wisdom and literary traditions, to illustrate the core principles of this approach.

The essay explores the concept of "incompleteness" as a generative force, challenging the academy's obsession with achieving a false sense of completeness and self-sufficiency. Through engaging narratives, the essay demonstrates how collaboration, mobility, and the exchange of knowledge are essential for individual and collective growth.

The dynamics of knowledge exchange are further analysed through the lens of metaphors such as the charging and discharging of a smartphone, highlighting the reciprocal nature of learning and the importance of continuous engagement with diverse perspectives.

The essay also critically examines the role of technology, particularly Artificial Intelligence (AI), in shaping the future of African scholarship and publishing. While acknowledging the potential of AI to enhance access and translation, it cautions against uncritical reliance on technological solutions, emphasising the enduring importance of human expertise, cultural nuance, and linguistic sensitivity, especially in the context of indigenous African languages.

Part III: Celebrating Pioneers: Indigenous Publishing and the Legacy of Henry Chakava

The book culminates in a tribute to the significant contributions of individuals who have played a pivotal role in transforming the African publishing landscape. It focuses on the legacy of Henry Chakava, a pioneering figure whose vision and dedication profoundly impacted the development of indigenous publishing in Kenya and beyond.

The essay examines Chakava's efforts to challenge the dominance of multinational corporations, promote African languages, and foster a more inclusive and representative literary environment. It highlights his crucial role in establishing key networks and initiatives that strengthened African writing, publishing, and book distribution.

However, this essay does not shy away from acknowledging the persistent challenges facing African publishing, including infrastructural limitations, economic constraints, and the ongoing struggle to achieve linguistic justice and cultural autonomy. It underscores the importance of building upon the foundation laid by pioneers like Chakava to create a sustainable and thriving publishing ecosystem that empowers African voices and ensures the wide dissemination of African knowledge.

In conclusion, this book offers a compelling and nuanced exploration of the past, present, and future of African scholarship and publishing. By weaving together theoretical frameworks, practical insights, and historical perspectives, it provides a valuable resource for scholars, publishers, policymakers, and anyone invested in the intellectual and cultural development of the African continent.

Part I
Reimagining African Scholarship: Politics of Knowledge and the Call for Conviviality

Transforming African Scholarly Writing: Politics of Knowledge Production, Mobility and Conviviality[1]

Abstract

This 2022 keynote lecture for the African Peacebuilding Network (APN) and Next Gen Fellows Virtual Writing and Dissemination workshop opens by asserting that African scholarship must fully acknowledge the global politics of knowledge production and consumption. While African scholarship, like all scholarship, necessitates rigour, scientific methods, contextual awareness, and critical appraisal, the specific focus on "African scholarly writing" is important because it has often been characterised by an outward gaze and subjected to internal and external pressures to conform to Eurocentric expectations and publication outlets. This is despite the growth of quality African publishing houses and the increased availability of their publications through creative partnerships and digital innovations.

Decolonisation, a persistent aspiration, requires Africans to stop downplaying, disparaging, and demeaning the familiar and local in favour of celebrating the distant and unfamiliar. Given that Africa is and always has been a continent on the move, research and writing about Africa and Africans must reflect this reality. Scholarship should move beyond simplistic, singular narratives to offer explanations of complex situations

[1] Updated from a keynote lecture initially presented at the 2022 APN and NEXT GEN Fellows Virtual Writing and Dissemination Workshop, March 14-16, 2022, and published as AFRICAN PEACEBUILDING NETWORK APN LECTURE SERIES: NO. 8, https://www.ssrc.org/publications/transforming-african-scholarly-writing-politics-of-knowledge-production-mobility-and-conviviality/, accessed 04 March 2025.

and provide insight into the everyday aspirations and encounters that shape African existence. This approach fosters the "convivial scholarship" that the continent needs and that its dynamic and intellectual people are uniquely positioned to produce. Developing this kind of scholarship requires moving beyond rigid conceptual, methodological, and analytical preconceptions, routines, and predictabilities, because they cannot do justice to a rapidly evolving subject matter. Participatory scholarship that embraces African mobilities will be well-equipped to develop innovative conceptual and methodological tools, enhancing our understanding of the nuanced complexities and composite nature of Africa and Africans in constant motion.

In essence, this lecture addresses the politics of knowledge production and consumption within African scholarship. It advocates for a "convivial scholarship" that recognises incompleteness, mobility, and the interconnectedness of knowledge. Furthermore, it critiques the tendency of African scholars to prioritise Western publication outlets and urges the decolonisation of African scholarship. Crucially, it emphasises the importance of scholarly work reflecting the dynamism and mobility of African people and cultures.

Introduction

Knowledge production in a world of the unacknowledged universality of incompleteness and mobility is not just a technical, professional, and presumably objective exercise to be confined to book publishers and peer review processes as impartial mediators. As used here, incompleteness is not an inadequacy to feel inferior about, but rather, a norm or disposition to recognise and provide for in our actions and interactions with fellow humans, and with the world out there, both real and imagined. Such recognition of incompleteness and provision for the cross-fertilisation of ideas should be within and between disciplines, and between researchers/

scholars/ academics and those outside the academy. As long as scholarship is undertaken in a world where the dominant template continues to be one of conquest, domination, and zero-sum games of superiority and supremacy, a world in which the universality of humanity is subjected to hierarchies of visibility and credibility, one can ill afford to ignore the politics and ethics of scholarly research, writing, publication, and consumption.

Context (social, cultural, economic, and historical) and interconnecting local and global power relations matter in what is produced and served up as scholarship, especially in a world stubbornly immersed in hierarchies of race, ethnicity, place, space, class, gender, sexuality, generation, mobility, belonging, and citizenship, to name just a few. A world fixated with ambitions of completeness, however illusory, de-emphasises the mutuality of debt and indebtedness, and denies the compositeness of being and belonging. It refuses to acknowledge and provide for the universality of incompleteness and mobility.

The sociology and ethnography of actual practices in knowledge production in and on Africa, I argue, are best understood by what I have described as convivial scholarship. This is a scholarship driven by the understanding that, as human beings, we are always in the process of becoming through encounters, interconnections, interdependencies, compositeness, and the mutuality of debt and indebtedness once we acknowledge and provide for our incompleteness and mobility. The argument is for convivial scholarship that is relevant, self-critical but not self-punishing, adaptive, reflexive, and attuned to the temporal and spatial contexts within which scholars write.

Scholarly Writing: Beyond Specification

Scholarly writing beyond specification is a craft that scholars are expected to nurture and develop. If writing, in general, is a craft, writing for scholarly publishing is particularly so. The pressure scholars come under to publish or perish means that often too many scholars are chasing after too few scholarly outlets – like journals and books. This renders scholarly publishing incredibly competitive, with the implication that many scholars might fall by the wayside even when they've got remarkably interesting research results to share with the wider scientific community. With opportunities come opportunisms, and the world of publishing is no exception to this dynamic.

Just as each research process is supposed to go through steps that include 1) choosing a scientifically and socially relevant topic and designing a research project; 2) determining the methods and data collection techniques; 3)operationalising the project; 4) analysing the data; 5) presenting the results; and 6) sharing the findings, so too is the scholar expected to explain the basic steps they followed to arrive at what they are now sharing with the wider scientific community. The emphasis is on a critical understanding of the values, assumptions, and motivations that underpin research cultures, traditions, and practices.

Just like in research, it helps in scholarly writing if authors can situate themselves in a given field, area of study, or discipline because that permits assessors and peer-reviewers to know what pool of basic assumptions or theoretical frameworks to draw from in making sense of the work they are called upon to evaluate. It also prevents the work from being judged using yardsticks that the authors never intended or with which they are not even familiar. In other words, if an author fails to say clearly that their writing is in the social sciences or the humanities, it is hardly surprising if someone in the natural sciences were to take the author to task for having or not having employed natural science theories and methods or methodologies. Similarly, a sociologist of religion who fails to situate their work clearly within the confines of the subdiscipline of sociology of religion should hardly be surprised if a physical geographer accuses them of not being sufficiently grounded in physical geography. Authors are of course encouraged to, when and where necessary, draw from various disciplinary backgrounds, approaches, or perspectives, provided they do so consciously and are aware of the possible implications on the assessment of their work. In other words, one writes for one's peers or a particular readership. One does not simply write like a fisherperson casting their net and hoping for the best.

Scholars have to be noticeably clear about the argument they want to make and, even more so, why they believe the argument is worth making. It is not because we are researching religion that we should assume we can get away with being dogmatic. Every assertion and every claim we make must be substantiated. From the outset, one should give an outline of the objectives of the proposed writing, stressing the theoretical/intellectual and practical/applied reasons for thinking the argument worth making, and clearly articulating how one intends to develop one's argument or basic assumptions.

A key dimension of scholarly writing is being able to relate what one writes to the body of literature relevant to the subject matter. One would therefore be able to answer the question of what other research, studies, writings, theories, and conclusions are relevant to one's proposed writing and how one intends to draw from the approaches and results of the works in question to inform and guide one's arguments in the writing. Such review of past and current literature of relevance should not simply be a list or inventory of research articles, reports, and books that the author considers appropriate (although relevant works need to be mentioned). It must lead to extrapolations of principles, concepts, themes, and orientations from these works that can be built into the author's own work and related to their overall theoretical interests, giving direction to their work.

A *critical appraisal* of a piece of research, published or otherwise, calls for:

a. Finding out the theoretical assumptions or frameworks under which the research was done and how generally familiar the author is with ongoing theoretical debates.
b. The methodology used by the author to collect their data. How convincing is this? Was this the best possible approach? Could further insight have been gained, had they employed another methodology?
c. What is the author's main argument? How original is it? How clearly do they make the argument, and how naturally does it flow from the body of data?
d. What contribution to knowledge does the work make? To what extent does it cover gaps, provide new insights, elucidate existing theories, break new grounds theoretically, etc.? To answer these questions satisfactorily requires deep immersion and familiarity with relevant and related literature.

To write meaningfully based on research is to demonstrate one's ability to make sense of the data one has collected. In research terminology, this means to analyse or seek to link the research findings to the research questions. It is worth bearing in mind that the answers to the questions should not be unrelated or separate fragments. Each answer should form an integral part of a larger whole – the researcher's overall design – and the researcher should have made sure of this from the outset. Ideally, the answer/data should be capable of being put together in a pattern within the framework of the design guided by the author's initial research objectives. This might sound too akin to hard sciences for those of us with social sciences and humanities pretensions, but, as I have argued elsewhere, the "methodic process of critical, systematic questioning, meticulous data gathering, analysis and interpretation, and alert receptiveness to the humility of doubt, the force of evidence, and the possibility of error" doesn't have to be confined to the natural or hard sciences (Nyamnjoh 2015: 49-50).

The analysis is not something that researchers start to think about after collecting their data. The analysis goes hand-in-hand with and stems from the preceding stages. Of course, post-hoc hypotheses, formulations, and analyses, particularly "the analysis of the unexpected," are not ruled out per se and, at times, can be very fruitful. But blind fishing expeditions for data (or groping in the dark without a roadmap or a clear sense of direction in the hope that something useful might turn up) are not encouraged. Moreover, this is not an economical way of proceeding. Time and resources are key in research, writing, and publishing. The research process should be systematic in its steps and considerations. The framework or outline of the analysis should be prepared before the data is collected and this can be done without straitjacketing the operation or stifling imaginative excursions.

Analysis and interpretation go hand in hand. Interpretation entails making sense of or reading meaning into the data a researcher has collected. It invites the researcher to explain (i.e., facilitate understanding of) the phenomenon being investigated. This requires the researcher to link or relate their findings to the hypothesis/basic assumptions and objectives set out at the beginning of the research. To what extent have these been validated? Does this call for a reformulation/ modification of or total break with existing theories? If a new theory is required, how would the researcher go about formulating it? In short, interpretation invites the researcher to link theory to fact and to show how interconnected and important they both are for the advancement of knowledge in their domain of research and scholarship.

Normally, research should yield new knowledge, which should be presented to the wider scholarly community of practice to which one belongs and is sustainably networked. The sharing can take place through multiple forms: research report, thesis, dissertation, film, documentary, public and/or policy discussion, interviews with journalists or peers, exposition/exhibition, blog post, podcast, social media posts, ethnographic novel, journal paper, book, book chapter, etc. Because those researched often have various and sometimes contradictory viewpoints on issues, it is important in presenting research findings to give the various social actors a voice in our texts, to quote them word verbatim (i.e., undoctored and unsanitised), sometimes extensively. Sometimes the researcher plays the referee between competing accounts or perspectives on the same issue, thereby bringing a certain hierarchy to bear on various discourses, in an effort to make meaningful their contradictions and incoherencies. In this regard and in the interest of theorisation, rich scholarly writing entails an investment in bringing Clifford Geertz's "thick description" (1973) into well-articulated and sustained conversation with John Jackson's "thin description," (2013) especially in a world of accelerated mobility of people and social media-driven circulation of cultures.

In most university settings, for students studying for a degree, the presentation of findings often takes the form of a monograph, which is a detailed account of the phenomenon being investigated and an interpretation of the facts to bring out the logics that underpin them. Whether writing a monograph, an article, or a book, writing offers the researcher an opportunity to review their understanding of an area and provides the reader with a guide to measure the researcher's knowledge and competence in that given area. Researchers should therefore use whatever they write as a focus for their reading, and as a device for sorting out their ideas about an issue. Publishers and readers expect a well-structured piece of writing, showing a critical awareness of the relevant literature, and an ability to summon arguments and evidence relevant to the subject matter. Scholarly writing demands a sustained presence of mind and generosity in drawing on and acknowledging the contributions of others to the subject matter.

In writing, a researcher must avoid making assertions without necessary evidence or arguments to support them. Publishers and readers are interested in the author's views and opinions, only to the extent that their writing is able to demonstrate how they arrived at them. It is easier to make a statement than to support it. In scholarly writing, one is expected to support statements, not simply to make them. Authors are expected to acknowledge by properly referencing all quotations or allusions to other people's work and even one's own work. It is a strength to write with the hope of reaching beyond one's echo chambers. However, within and beyond one's echo chambers, belief and trust are likely to stand in the way of truth, especially when the truth is critical of or counter to conventional wisdom and practice.

Why the prefix "African" in Scholarly Writing?

What has Africa got to do with it? Is there anything in scholarly writing that is distinctively African, apart from the aspiration that African scholars who invest in writing with "the accepted template" have to share their work and contribute to global debates? Collectively, Africans are increasing the number of books they publish with established and renowned publishers and the number of articles they publish in top or highly ranked journals from Africa and beyond. These efforts improve the visibility of knowledge produced in Africa as a geographical location in an otherwise standardised, homogenised, routinised, and predictable global marketplace of scholarship. Isn't it enough to simply publish according to internationally established and globally shared standards of excellence in scholarship? What is it about an African scholar, beyond the imperative to publish, that should compel or urge them to write? And does that call for more than just generalities and the technicalities of writing? Put differently, what matters more: content or technique? Message or messenger? Or is it a question of seeking a careful balance between the two? What would an African balance between content and technique, message and messenger, look like? And what changes to publications policies and practices would that necessitate?

Although scholarly writing is part of a globally shared repertoire of scholarship, it is understood that context shapes scholarship and the perspectives of scholars. This should caution against a propensity to settle for scholarship by analogy or mimicry. Such scholarship, like racism in the following statement by Toni Morrison, can be a distraction:

> "The very serious function of racism … is distraction. It keeps you from doing your work. It keeps you explaining, over and over again, your reason for being. Somebody says you have no language and so you spend 20 years proving that you do. Somebody says your head isn't shaped properly so you have scientists working on the fact that it is. Somebody says that you have no art so you dredge that up. Somebody says that you have no kingdoms and so you dredge that up. None of that is necessary." ("A Humanist View," a 1975 speech Toni Morrison gave at Portland State University)[2]

---

[2] See "12 of Toni Morrison's Most Memorable Quotes", https://www.nytimes.com/2019/08/06/books/toni-morrison-quotes.html, accessed 05 March 2022.

Knowledge production and scholarly publishing are steeped in political and cultural considerations and influenced by hierarchies of being and becoming, which shape and colour perceptions and relationships. This poses a challenge of how to navigate the politics of knowledge production and dissemination informed by unequal encounters, unequal relationships, and competing traditions of knowing and meaning-making. Concepts, methods, and debates must not be rushed into a universal currency or canon in the heterogeneous global knowledge market or community before they have been tested and scrutinised in different geographies and by people of different racial, ethnic, cultural, class, gender, sexual, and generational identities. For Africa, this means that knowledge is shallow if the process fails to include relevant sensitivities, sensibilities, perspectives, and scholars who claim or are claimed by Africa on the continent and beyond.

This consideration was at the heart of the creation of the Council for the Development of Social Science Research in Africa (CODESRIA) in 1973. The creation of CODESRIA was also partly motivated by a perceived need for greater recognition and representation of what African social scientists had to offer in debates where they were often reduced to passive observers whose role was to implement and not to think. The high rejection rate for African scholarship in Northern journals meant that African scholars essentially had to choose between bending over backward to accommodate debates in colonial languages, whose origins and assumptions differed from the burning questions and concerns of their continent, or create and sustain alternative outlets for their research informed by greater relevance in theory and practice the diverse expectations and aspirations of Africans.

The situation was compounded by the fact that African scholars tended to operate in linguistic silos and echo chambers determined by the colonial languages (English, French, Portuguese, Spanish, and German) they had inherited and the fact that what existed as scholarship in one of the languages was hardly available in translation in the others. This alarming incongruence between experience and mode of representation begs ongoing inquiry and contemplation because, alas, the asymmetries that CODESRIA was meant to address remain largely in place, despite its formidable efforts to make a difference. Providing for strong publications and dissemination in its programs was a clear indication that the founders of CODESRIA as a pan-African organisation opted for significant independence of thought and scholarship – even if these continued to be articulated in colonial languages and dependent on donor (largely western) funding[3] – as well as critical engagement with Africa on the continent and in the diaspora.

CODESRIA has, since 1973, established itself as a leading scholarly publisher in the social sciences and humanities on the African continent, with 90 percent of what it publishes correlating to the research and activities it sponsors among various research networks in universities and research institutes throughout the continent and, increasingly, in the diaspora. Since 2000, CODESRIA has regularly published – in collaboration with scholarly professional associations in most cases – six bilingual (usually in French and English with the occasional article in Portuguese) and a few multilingual journals. In many regards, CODESRIA has been a lone voice in making a case for the African value-add in scholarly publishing and in resisting takeover and commercialisation by Western publishing. Universities, research institutes, and other professional scholarly

[3] Some could argue that such dependence on funding by western donors, however justified, stood in contradiction to CODESRIA's decolonisation project and the pursuit of Pan-Africanism and intellectual freedom.

associations on the continent are only too willing to hand over publication and control of their journals to the Western publishing entrepreneurs fishing for profits.

I worked with CODESRIA from 2003 to 2009 as its head of publications and dissemination. There I came to understand how easily one could publish in and on Africa and perish (Nyamnjoh 2004). This was not only vis-à-vis the external world where it is more fashionable to write and read about Africa through Western prisms and from non-African sources. It was also, more painfully, a regular experience that many scholars on the continent applying to participate in CODESRIA activities (conferences, workshops, seminars, methodology, and themed institutes) seldom engaged and referenced CODESRIA publications. This was the case despite the dedicated efforts of CODICE, the CODESRIA documentation service, to source and make documentary resources available to its membership. The reason for this was not only the inaccessibility of CODESRIA publications in many parts of the continent because of distribution challenges. It was also because scholars in Africa learn and become adept at playing the game of hierarchy of credibility informed by where one is published, with Western publishers and publications almost a priori given preferential positionings higher up the hierarchy, if not quite simply at the apex. African publishers, CODESRIA included, are defined by African scholars seeking local and international visibility and credentialism as local by default, while publishers outside of the continent, especially when located in the West, stand a particularly good chance to be defined as international, and therefore as more prestigious and high impact. It doesn't seem to matter that African nation-states otherwise tend to rigidly police their borders against the flexible mobility of Africans in an effort to contain what they term "inter-national migration". Pan-Africanism, it would appear, is at best opportunistic and selective. As chair of Langaa Research and Publications in Cameroon, a country with no active university press, I often receive feedback from local professors who acknowledge the quality of publications by Langaa but who lament the fact that the publisher's address is in "little known Bamenda." "If only Langaa could acquire an American address" (even if by identifying a co-publisher there), I am sometimes told, "Langaa would be the place to publish."

Back to publishing in Africa. In a publishing landscape where geography and prestige often overshadow content, the struggle for Indigenous language publishing in Africa is stark. Writing in 1977, using Kenya as an example, Henry Chakava, then Managing Director, Heinemann Educational Books for East African, identified the challenges of publishing in African languages to include: "considerable local variation … while dealing with the same language", with many of the languages lacking a standard orthography. Thus, "a decision to publish in an African language at once involves one in problems of evolving additional signs and symbols" and designing new fonts that "makes the final product difficult to read". "Technically, and from a production point of view, it also means a limitation in the choice of authors, readers, editors, and even printers – who will be drawn from the particular ethnic group to whom the book is addressed." That was in 1977 (Chakava 1977).

Chakava passed away in March 2024. I wonder what he would have said has changed since then, in African language publishing, especially with the avalanche of decolonial scholarship that we have witnessed. As the saying goes, one must walk the talk to be taken seriously. Sterile prescriptiveness amounts to little. It contradicts the popular rhetoric of decolonisation. Even when the orthography has been standardised and the right signs and symbols developed, publishing in indigenous African languages has not blossomed.

South Africa's Lovedale Press, established in 1823, exemplifies this struggle.

Within such a hierarchy of credibility in which geography and prestige matter more than content and contradict the decoloniality/decolonisation rhetoric and bandwagonism, it is hardly surprising that publishing in indigenous and endogenous languages is either non-existent or acutely underdeveloped throughout the African continent. In South Africa for example, efforts were underway in 2024 to revive "Lovedale Press … established as a small printing press in 1823 by the Glasgow Missionary Society", with a focus on publishing "evangelical and educational material" in isiXhosa. Lovedale Press "provided a vehicle for black authors to publish their work and was a pioneer in printing African literature", and trained "Black South Africans … as apprentices in printing and bookbinding". Even the words on a plaque at the entrance of Lovedale Press, by famous Xhosa author AC Jordan, who published many books through the press – "The earliest record of anything written by any Bantu-speaking African in his own language in South Africa was made at the small printing press at Old Lovedale." – could not save it from bankruptcy and debts. It's last publication was a primary school reader – *Unxibelelwano Olululo Lwesixhosa* – in 2015. Lovedale Press "was auctioned off to 18 former employees in 2001, and the building was sold." Reportedly, efforts are underway since late 2023 by the Thabo Mbeki Foundation, in collaboration with Rhodes University, Walter Sisulu University, Fort Hare University, and Nelson Mandela University, to revive and re-imagine the Lovedale Press. If this rescue mission bears fruit, it would serve to salvage Lovedale's contribution to education, religion, culture and literature in South

Africa through the prism of Black South African authors, printers and bookbinders.[4]

Mohammed Umar, founder of Salaam Publishing, offers a compelling example of the potential – and the challenges – of publishing in Indigenous African languages. He's passionately committed to making his books accessible to a wide audience, translating his novels and children's stories into a remarkable number of languages. Imagine:

> *Samad in the Forest* is available in a staggering 111 African languages!
>
> *Samad in the Desert* can be enjoyed in 36 languages.
>
> *A Trip to the Zoo* and *The Circle of Life* each come in 17 languages.
>
> *Amina* is available in 4 languages.
>
> Despite the logistical hurdles and the limited market for these books, Umar persists. He believes in the power of Indigenous languages and hopes that African leaders, scholars, and bookstores will join him in championing this vital aspect of cultural preservation.[5]

The artificial intelligence revolution holds immense potential for the future of indigenous language publishing and translation, but it's crucial to approach this technology with a nuanced perspective. The experience of author Mohammed Umar offers valuable insights. In an email exchange about AI translation, he shared his observations:

> When an advanced AI was used to translate two of my stories, I gathered feedback from readers worldwide.

---

[4] Sandiso Phaliso, "Reviving history: Thabo Mbeki Foundation aims to restore Eastern Cape's 200-year-old Lovedale Press", https://www.news24.com/life/books/reviving-history-thabo-mbeki-foundation-aims-to-restore-eastern-capes-200-year-old-lovedale-press-20240606, accessed 07 June 2024.

[5] Mohammed Umar, interviewed, December 30, 2024. See also, https://www.salaampublishing.com/about.html

> For European and other standardised languages, the accuracy was around 70-80%. However, for remote languages in Africa, Asia, and South America, where standardisation is less developed, the quality was significantly lower.
>
> Even in standardised languages, AI lacks the nuances of human translation. Its vocabulary is limited and often misses the mark. For instance, in the Hausa translation, the AI consistently chose words I wouldn't have used, sometimes opting for terms that are rarely employed in natural conversation.
>
> For my book *Samad in the Forest*, I wanted to add a Kanuri edition. I sent an AI-generated translation to a Kanuri language professor at the University of Maiduguri for review. He found it laughable. He provided his own translation, and the difference between human and machine translation was stark. The AI made numerous errors, such as translating 'crocodile' as 'bird' and failing to distinguish between 'baboon' and 'monkey.'
>
> I've heard similar complaints from others, particularly in Africa and South America. AI struggles with translating terms like 'crocodile' in many indigenous languages.[6]

Umar's experience highlights the limitations of current AI translation for indigenous languages. While AI can be a useful tool, it requires careful human oversight and should not be seen as a replacement for skilled human translators. The nuances of language, culture, and context are crucial elements that AI still struggles to grasp, underscoring the vital role of human expertise in preserving and promoting linguistic diversity.

In conclusion, the struggle for Indigenous language publishing in Africa continues. Despite the challenges, there are individuals and organisations dedicated to promoting and preserving African languages through publishing.

---

[6] Mohammed Umar, interviewed, January 6, 2025.

It doesn't seem to matter that with improved distribution of scholarly content by African publishers thanks to technological developments in digital publishing and dissemination (such as Print-on-Demand and e-books) and to distribution initiatives championed by distributors such as African Books Collective (ABC), African publishers have become more competitive and their content more accessible and discoverable on distribution platforms and vendors such as Project MUSE, JSTOR, ProQuest and ESBCO[7], as well as on Goodreads, Amazon, and Google.

African Books Collective is an "African-owned, worldwide marketing and distribution outlet" for books from Africa. Over 100 publishers in over 20 countries across Africa participate in the collective. They share a common ethos of publishing from within African cultures and asserting Africa's voice in Africa and internationally. Participating publishers focus on scholarly and literary works including some children's books and comprise research institutes, university presses, commercial presses, nongovernment organisations (NGOs), and writers' organisations. The collective is owned by its founder publishers, who elect a five-member Council of Management that meets annually. The Council is responsible "for setting the collective's strategy and for its representation in the wider book and publishing world." ABC "seeks to be profit-making on behalf of its publishers and is non-profit making on its own behalf." The ABC website lists its top titles in 2020 (from Tanzania, Ghana, Zimbabwe, Kenya, Cameroon, and Rwanda). In 2022,

---

[7] See "University press selection of e-book vendors for US academic libraries: Why work with X but not Y?" by Mei Zhang (2022), *Learned Publishing*, http://doi:10.1002/leap.1447, on how these "big four" vendors of scholarly content by university presses dominate the e-book market globally. Also see: www.statista.com/statistics/715001/preferred-e-book-vendors-at-academic-libraries-in-us

the ABC was distributing over 3000 books.[8] Beyond the initial surprise it provokes, the location of ABC in Oxford is evidence of Africa's reality as a dancing masquerade with which we must keep pace to be best situated to depict its creative nimble-footedness and encounters.

A growing number of Northern audiences whose attention we crave in our scholarly endeavours, increasingly aware of the gaps produced by previous systems and enduring hierarchies, seem to be supportive of helping to fill them by encouraging the dissemination and consumption of African scholarship published by African publishers.

African scholars and university bureaucracies understand "International publishers" to be publishers situated outside of the continent. They credit such publishers with rigorous peer review mechanisms, professional standards, and a capacity to attract greater visibility for their publications than any African publisher can. This occurs even when the scholars in question are on the editorial boards and active as peer reviewers for the African publishers they disparage. By extension, they disparage their own institutions based in Africa. Disparaging African publishers simply because they are in Africa extends to disparaging African research institutions and universities themselves because they are based on the continent of Africa. This amounts to rituals of self-flagellation. Interestingly, having studied rituals of flagellation

---

[8] See www.africanbookscollective.com/about-us. Also see "Interview with Justin Cox, CEO, African Books Collective," by Olatoun Gabi-Williams (2020), www.academia.edu/42000363/Interview_with_Justin_Cox_CEO_African_Books_Collective; and, Justin Cox, "African Books Collective: 30 Years of Providing Visibility for African Books in the Global Market Place" https://www.readafricanbooks.com/opinion/30-years-of-providing-visibility-for-african-books-in-the-global-market-place/, accessed 05 March 2022.

among the so-called "primitive" societies for centuries, some scholars have become so fond of self-flagellation that they adore everything foreign or "international" and intensely hate everything about themselves. This brings to mind the story of a Cameroonian patient at a hospital, who vigorously protested when the doctor suggested administering a "local anaesthesia," insisting that she wanted absolutely nothing short of an "imported anaesthesia."

There are, increasingly, Africans committed to publishing in Africa. The dominant situation, however, is one in which, if and when African scholars approach African publishers with submissions, these are likely to be manuscripts that have been rejected by their international publishers of preference. In some instances, the affliction to "whiten up" is so acute that they would rather publish with vanity presses and predatory publishers outside of the continent and thus international in their estimation than publish with a remotely reputable publisher on the continent. The impact of latest information and communication technologies on the global availability and accessibility of publications by African scholarly outlets does not appear to affect this attitude in any significant way. A consequence of such a situation is that the quality of a book or an article no longer depends on its contents and what peer reviewers as critical consumers have to say, but rather on its publishers and what university promotion committees attribute as "international" and "local" publishers. It is all too common, in many a country, for established professors to delay the academic progress of younger colleagues because the latter have published locally. Hardly is the focus primarily on the content of what has been published and seldom is the development of next-generation scholars appreciated.

Sometimes a publisher in Europe and North America loses its visibility and status in the eyes of African scholars for no other reason but the fact that it is owned and operated by a member of the African diaspora. It would appear, thus, that our quarrel is much more with ourselves, and the excruciating self-doubt that inhabits us, than with publishers and their professionalism as such. Reading for knowledge and substance has easily been replaced by guesswork and the art of keeping up appearances. This is not to deny that, even in the West, the systems for evaluating publications score journal articles in area studies lower than articles published in journals that are known to be at the cutting edge of the disciplines, just as articles published in non-English language outlets get lower scores than English language outlets.

In terms of the decolonisation imperative, it appears that, even as African scholars are critical of knowledge produced in accordance with Eurocentric canons and epistemic values, they are ready to absolve Western publishers and their editorial processes, as long as they are accorded visibility and credibility, even if not on their terms as decolonial scholars. Beyond symbolic deconstruction and critique of the politics of knowledge, decolonisation, and transformation, it would appear such actions are seldom about rupture or making good bedfellows of one's rhetoric and actions. They are about creating space for a complementary politics of inclusion within the prevailing framework, templates and standards of visibility, legitimation, and credentialism. African scholars who critically question the status quo are summarily condemned as "disruptive" by academic gendarmes (high priests or gatekeepers) anxious to police the status quo. If our aim is to reconcile scholarly excellence with relevance to the African context, we can hardly content ourselves with merely aspiring to increase the number of articles and books we publish in top or highly ranked "international" journals and with top international publishers. We ought to be driven preponderantly by an understanding in relation to Africa that not all that counts can be counted and not all that can be counted counts. We must make our scholarship count for the valorisation of Africa beyond tokenism. This, of course, should not amount to sacrificing excellence for relevance, and quality for mediocrity.

We can't simply lend ourselves as tools in the production of knowledge that is all about downplaying, disparaging, or demeaning the familiar and the local and celebrating the unfamiliar, especially when one has been schooled to internalise and reproduce Europe and its global ambitions of dominance through the dedicated pursuit of whitening up. In such a process, not much thought is given to the fact that being local or international is not confined to any particular location but is always a function of position and perspective vis-à-vis the reality at hand. To a child born and brought up in Oxford or Cambridge for example, Oxford and Cambridge university presses are first and foremost local publishers before being international, thanks to the colonial and imperial logics that sought to impress upon the rest of the world that the British were the world's finest race and God's best gift to humankind. Self-belief and a solid sense of self-worth would go a long way in disabusing ourselves of the obsession with whitening up. What if Africans were to rethink and revalorise our creative endeavours? For more on this subject, you might want to read two articles of mine, published in 2004 and 2012 respectively (Nyamnjoh 2004, 2012).

Dancing the Dance of Others and Related Metaphors

As a child, I was fed many a story of my maternal grandmother by those who knew her well. One of the stories that has stuck with me is the story of her as a consummate dancer without a dance of her own. At social gatherings, she spent her time impersonating others and imitating the way they danced. Often it was to ridicule the way others danced, but sometimes it was in approval. The result was that a party or event would start and end without others getting to know and appreciate what exactly, beyond imitating or mimicking others, was my grandmother's personal dance style. The lady who told this story, a contemporary of my grandmother, said she died without anyone ever knowing her dance. She had lived her life as a perfect copier and an astute performer of the art of others. She had earned distinction, the way an actor would do in Hollywood and be rewarded with an Oscars, by playing others. This is not to say playing others is not a worthwhile pursuit, especially if one does it as convincingly as did my grandmother. Not everyone has to be a scriptwriter. And, in any case, who says scriptwriting or original designer of something is better than the imitator? Sometimes the imitator does it better than the original designer.

In terms of the theme of our workshop, my grandmother was like a writer who was outstanding at literature reviews and did not share a story of her own to add value to such overviews of the creative outputs of others. A good literature review is one tailored to drive a research question or curiosity in a given area of interest to the researcher in question. Perhaps my grandmother's ambition was merely to entertain herself and those around her with the dances of others, to the point of losing herself wholly into them. In this respect, she could strike some as a dancer with so much to display but so little to hang onto. Her art of dancing could be likened to the salespersonship of someone with little knowledge or more than an ephemeral experience of what they are trying to persuade others to buy.

Some could argue that, as far as dancing was concerned, my grandmother never went beyond the stage of mimicry or hapless reproduction of others, even when she appeared to make fun of them. To be fair to her, she wasn't there to explain her motives when this story was told, so we can only guess what light she might have shed on the situation. Was my grandmother around to explain herself, she could perhaps have said that her desire was nothing more than to study, carefully, objectively, the dance styles of others, and never to reveal herself. Such a response would translate to what passes for a value-free science that appeals to the researcher to keep their subjectivities in check.

Scholarly writing is also about the making and remaking of intellectual and academic traditions. We should thus engage scholars of Africa in intellectual intergenerational biographical conversations while they are still alive, so they can justify their actions if need be. This is something I have encouraged as chair of the Langaa Research and publishing group, which has its home in Cameroon. As the next generation of African scholars, if you come across a book or an article on Africa that leaves you with more questions than answers, do not hesitate to find the contact details of the author and address your concerns to them, in the interest of promoting the cross-boundary conversations that we need.

Why we study and write about particular contexts should dictate *what* and *how* we study and write about those contexts. If our business is to decolonise or contribute to the engineering of social change and provide for the silences in the dances of the world, then we need to go behind the stage of the dances and dancers featured in public arenas and other places and spaces of visibility, almost as if they were the canon.

We need to focus on bringing Africanness to the attention of those who have been repeatedly served the dances of others, as if they had no dance of their own or as if their dances do not qualify to be the object of appreciation (Nyamnjoh 2016). As Chinua Achebe would put it, we should proceed in a manner that recognises and provides for the lion – as hunted or as hunter – telling its own story, in its own voice and style, and not necessarily in the zero-sum manner of the hunter in his quest for recognition and celebration among his trophy-hunter folk. The Africans we research and write about should be able to read and approve our accounts of them because we have resisted the temptation to caricature their predicaments in the interest of the monolithic pretensions of the ivory towers we are systematically invited to in the name of scholarship (Nyamnjoh 2017a).

To those of us overly eager to proliferate the world with our monologues and single stories, it is worth reminding ourselves that, to quote Okot p'Bitek on the Acholi, "every individual is an artist," even if "some are greater than others" (p'Bitek 1986: 35 & 41). There is no such thing as the perfect artist whom others should feel honoured to copy uncritically. Using the wisdom of proverbs, Chinua Achebe urges us as knowledge producers in a world of colonial prescriptiveness to bear in mind that "every community has enough firewood in its own forests for all the cooking it needs to do" (Achebe 2000: 7), and that "no man should enter his house through another man's gate." (Achebe 2000: 17). The historian Joseph Ki-Zerbo echoes the sentiment by reminding us of the indignity of sleeping on someone else's mat. To graduate or break free of Eurocentrism and the uneasy comfort of sleeping on "the mat of others" (*la natte des autres*), Ki-Zerbo calls on Africans to invest in self-knowledge and in scholarship informed by African experiences and perspectives (1992). To NoViolet Bulawayo, just as imagination is at the heart of freedom – "We have to insist on imagining the worlds that we want to see" – so too is what and who we write about a deliberate choice. For her, the choice is to write about those at the margins, who are in jeopardy of being sidestepped and rendered voiceless and invisible by poverty and the impunities of the powerful.[9]

[9] See Abdi Latif Dahir, "NoViolet Bulawayo Believes Freedom Begins With Imagination", March 2, 2022,

As Chimamanda Ngozi Adichie puts it in her caution against "the danger of a single story," it is from reading Chinua Achebe's books, that "I realised that people like me, girls with skin the colour of chocolate, whose kinky hair could not form ponytails, could also exist in literature."[10] And she went on to bring to life relatable people like her in her writing. Her short story, "The Headstrong Historian"[11] is an excellent example of the nuanced multivocality needed in representing the complexity of identities forged from the navigation and negotiation of myriad encounters by Africans in and out of the continent. Writers and artists, it would appear, have a thing or two to share with scholars and academics on how to go about the business of valorising African experiences and dynamism with required complexity and nuance.

Writing Africa and Africans as a Continent and People in Motion

How we research and write about Africa and Africans must reflect the reality of a continent and people on the move within and beyond the confines of geography. Everything moves – people, things, and ideas – in predictable and unpredictable ways. It should not surprise us that Africa moves and has always moved. If the deep historical conviction that Africa is the cradle of humankind holds, then everyone,

---

https://www.nytimes.com/2022/03/02/books/noviolet-bulawayo-glory.html, accessed 07 March 2022.

[10] Adichie CN (2009) The Dangers of a Single Story. Available at: www.ted.com/talks/chimamanda_adichie_the_danger_of_a_single_story.htm (accessed 21 March 2011)

[11] Chimamanda Ngozi Adichie, "The Headstrong Historian", June 16, 2008, https://www.newyorker.com/magazine/2008/06/23/the-headstrong-historian (accessed 07 March 2022)

regardless of their present location in the world, is African, or, at the very least, once was African.

The circulation of things, ideas, and people is not the monopoly of any group, community, society, or category of human. Mobility and circulation lead to encounters of various forms, encounters that define and redefine in myriad ways. If Africans, their belongings, and their ideas circulate, it follows that their identities, personal or collective, move as well. They move, among other things, through the stories they tell and the representations we as scholars make of them in what we research, write and publish.

Through encounters with others, mobile Africans are constantly navigating, negotiating, accommodating, or rejecting difference (in things, ideas, practices, and relations) in an open-ended manner that makes them permanent works in progress. Put differently, and seen through the prism of histories of mobility, identities (even when claimed exclusively and in the singular) are always composite and open-ended. No mobility or interaction, whether horizontal, vertical, or circular in nature, leaves anyone, anything, or any idea indifferent, even if it does not always result in immediate or tangible change.

As researchers of Africa and Africans on the move, we would agree that no encounter results in uncontested domination or total passivity. Some people may wilt in the face of domination, some resist it fervently, and others navigate and negotiate the tensions and contradictions brought about by the reality of domination in complex, creative, and innovative ways. Such creative and oftentimes circuitous navigation may hold potential for new and more convivial forms of identity, practice, and relating. If our scholarship is sensitive to and provides for such mobilities, it is well-placed to develop innovative conceptual and methodological tools to enhance understandings of the nuanced complexities that being and becoming African in motion engenders.

A Scholarship of Compositeness and Conviviality

In one of his proverbs, Chinua Achebe likens the world to a dancing masquerade, adding that if one wants to see it well, one can ill-afford to stand in one place. In other words, one cannot do justice to a fast-moving subject matter by staying glued to the same conceptual, methodological, and analytical preconceptions, routinisations, and predictabilities. Granted that Africa and Africans are permanently on the move, let me adopt and adapt Achebe's proverb to read: "Africa is like a mask dancing. If you want to see it well you do not stand in one place." This speaks of Africans as well: "Africans are like masks dancing. If you want to see them well you do not stand in one place." Nimble-footed realities require nimble-minded intellects and nimble-minded scholarship. Nimble-minded intellects need to bring historical ethnography into conversation with the ethnographic present. They need to draw on and distil from yesterday and today to inform a far-from-linear future. Let's draw on and adapt Achebe yet again: "Disciplines and scholarship are like masks dancing. If you want to see them well you do not stand in one place." The sort of scholarship this awareness of the universality of incompleteness and of mobility calls for is a scholarship of compositeness and conviviality (Nyamnjoh 2020).

Recognising interconnections and interdependence and promoting collaboration enriches scholarship. For the researcher, this means co-elaboration, co-investigation, co-production, and co-provision for the compositeness of being that acknowledges the outsider within and the insider without as intimate strangers. Convivial scholarship requires making a deliberate effort to reach in, identify, contemplate, understand, embrace, and become intimate with the stranger within us, in individuals, societies, disciplines, and fields of study alike. Such recognition of incompleteness and provision for the cross-fertilisation of ideas through mobility and encounters should be within and between disciplines, and between researchers/ scholars/ academics and those outside the academy whose lived realities inform or *ought* to inform knowledge production and consumption.

As researchers in and of Africa and Africans in their mobilities, we have the audacity and power to challenge and rethink knowledge production. We can promote and demand the imperatives of seeing, hearing, feeling, touching, and smelling the world from different angles, different vantage points, diverse backgrounds, different orientations, different perspectives, and different interests, as suggested by Chinua Achebe in his proverb about the dancing mask. Such conviviality in our scholarship should accommodate the likes of my grandmother who excelled at the dances of others, while simultaneously challenging members of her community to reactivate and bring into conversation their own distinctive creativity and innovation in dance. Imagine knowledge production as truly participatory, a process in which no race, gender, culture, ethnic or age group, geography, or any other social category has a monopoly.

Truly convivial scholarship does not seek, the way conventional debates on Africa and the disciplines from the vantage point of the powerful have, to define and confine by ignoring the facts, massaging them, or outrightly dictating what the facts should be. Rather than describing and limiting Africans in relation to territories, geographies, racial and ethnic categories, classes, genders, generations, religions, colonial linguistic spheres, or whatever other identity marker is in vogue, convivial scholarship should provide for the compositeness of being and becoming African as a permanent work in progress. If the call for conviviality, inclusion, multi-layeredness, and compositeness of being and relating is to be more than just a free for all, everything goes, hotchpotch of views and perspectives, convivial scholarship must challenge the academy to embrace and use the same critical consciousness that supposedly engendered the disciplines, their canons and their logics of practice, in contesting and transcending unproductive fixations with disciplinary boundaries and credos. Convivial scholarship confronts and humbles the challenge of over-prescription, over-standardisation, and over-prediction – in short, it seeks to undo the McDonaldisation of the disciplines and the compulsion for African scholars to whiten up through a scholarship of mimicry and analogy.

Convivial scholarship disrupts and subverts standardised and routinised reproduction of disciplinary structures of power and privilege, structures that scare away humility, curiosity, reflection, open-mindedness, and creative renewal. It advocates the combination of disciplinary depth and sharpness with open-minded critical consciousness and inclusivity in approach. It is critical and evidence-based, without limiting evidence to sensory perception or a fixation with predictability, generalisations, and teleology. Rather, it seeks to reconcile predictability with interpretability and is critical about sources and McDonaldised ideas of evidence. It is a scholarship that sees the human in the natural and the super-sensory, the local in the global and the global in the local. It provides for the dancer in the dance and the dance in the dancer.

Convivial scholarship brings seeming disparities into informed conversations, which do not ignore the hierarchies and power relations at play at both micro and macro levels of being and becoming. Rather, it draws attention to the histories and sociologies of violence and violation that create illusions of supremacy and zero-sum ambitions of conquest. Convivial scholarship challenges us – however grounded we may be in our disciplines and their logics of practice – to cultivate the disposition to be present and to be present everywhere at the same time, through others and by means of technologies of self-extension.

The capacity for presence in simultaneous multiplicities is attainable and sharpened through a recognition of and provision for compositeness of being. It is also sharpened by the capacity of disciplinary practitioners to accommodate disciplinary outsiders as a way of affording disciplinary insiders the opportunity to spread their wings and renew their canons. Convivial scholarship cautions disciplines, their borders, and gatekeepers to open up and creatively embrace difference and dynamism. It insists on an openness to the sensitivities and sensibilities that our compositeness of being imbues in us as students of society, such that we can do justice to the subjectivities of the composite "others" whose sociality we seek to understand and represent in our scholarship. With convivial scholarship, there are no final answers. Only permanent questions and ever exciting new angles of questioning. Such scholarship is predicated upon recognising and providing for incompleteness as a necessary attribute of being, from persons to disciplines and traditions of knowing and knowledge making (Nyamnjoh 2019, 2020, 2024).

I challenge us all, as scholars of Africa and Africans in motion, to research and write Africa and Africans through the prism of convivial scholarship.

Conclusion

This lecture concludes by firmly advocating for a transformative shift towards what it defines as "convivial scholarship" within African studies. This paradigm shift is essential for navigating the complex terrain of knowledge production and consumption, particularly in relation to Africa. Convivial scholarship necessitates a fundamental acknowledgment of the inherent incompleteness of knowledge and the dynamic, mobile nature of African identities and experiences. It champions the value of interconnectedness, interdependence, and vigorous collaboration, actively promoting the inclusion of diverse voices from within and outside traditional academic circles. Furthermore, it demands a critical consciousness that fearlessly challenges established disciplinary boundaries, inherent power structures, and the persistent pressure on African scholars to conform to Eurocentric norms and expectations. In essence, the lecture has made a passionate calls for a decolonised and radically dynamic approach to African scholarship. This approach must be self-reflective, contextually relevant, and deeply engaged with the rich and varied lived experiences of Africans, accurately mirroring the continent's and its people's dynamism and mobility (Nyamnjoh (2017b[2015]).

References

Achebe, C. (2000) *Home and Exile*. New York: Anchor Books.

Chakava, H. (1977) "Publishing in a Multilingual Situation: the Kenya case", *The African Book Record*, vol. 3, no. 2, 1977, pp. 83-90. https://doi.org/10.1515/abpr.1977.3.2.83.

Geertz, C. (1973) "Thick description: Toward an interpretive theory of culture", in *The Interpretation of Cultures*. New York: Basic Books. pp. 3-30.

Jackson, J. L. (2013) *Thin Description: Ethnography and the African Hebrew Israelites of Jerusalem*, Cambridge Massachusetts: Harvard University Press.

Ki-Zerbo J (ed.) (1992) *Le Développement Clès en Tête. La natte des autres: Pour un développement endogène en Afrique* [The Key to Development. The Mat of Others. A Case for Endogenous Development in Africa]. Dakar: CODESRIA, 1–71.

Nyamnjoh, F. B. (2004) "From Publish or Perish to Publish and Perish: What 'Africa's 100 Best Books'

Tell Us About Publishing Africa", *Journal of Asian and African Studies*, Vol.39(5):331-355.

Nyamnjoh, F. B. (2012) "Potted Plants in Greenhouses: A Critical Reflection on the Resilience of Colonial Education in Africa," *Journal of Asian and African Studies*, Vol.47(2):129-154.

Nyamnjoh, F. B. (2015) "Beyond an Evangelizing Public Anthropology: Science, Theory and Commitment," *Journal of Contemporary African Studies*, 33(1): 48-63.

Nyamnjoh, F. B. (2016) *#RhodesMustFall: Nibbling at Resilient Colonialism in South Afric*a, Bamenda: Langaa.

Nyamnjoh, F. B. (2017a) *Drinking from the Cosmic Gourd: How Amos Tutuola Can Change Our Minds*, Bamenda: Langaa.

Nyamnjoh, F. B. (2017b[2015]) "Incompleteness: Frontier Africa and the Currency of Conviviality," in: *Journal of Asian and African Studies*. 52(3): 253-270.

Nyamnjoh, F.B. (2019) "Decolonizing the University in Africa," *Oxford Research Encyclopedias*, Oxford University Press,
DOI: 10.1093/acrefore/9780190228637.013.717, pp.1-36.

Nyamnjoh, F. B. (2020) *Decolonising the Academy: A Case for Convivial Scholarship* (Carl Schlettwein Lecture 14), Basel: Basler Afrika.

Nyamnjoh, F. B. (2024) *Incompleteness, Mobility and Conviviality: Ad. E. Jensen Memorial Lectures 2023 Frobenius-Institut, Goethe-University*, Bamenda: Langaa.

p'Bitek, O. (1986) *Artist the Ruler: Essays on Art, Culture and Values*. Nairobi: East African Educational Publishers. Pp. 35 & 41.

Part II
Embracing Incompleteness: Metaphors, Mobility, and the Dynamics of Knowledge Exchange

Reimagining African Scholarship: A Convivial Approach[1]

Abstract

The keynote address "Reimagining African Scholarship: A Convivial Approach" challenges the conventional norms of African knowledge production. It critiques the prevailing focus on criticism and the imposition of external solutions, advocating instead for a collaborative and inclusive model of scholarship. The address emphasises the importance of dialogue, mobility, and the integration of diverse knowledge systems, including indigenous traditions. It challenges the pursuit of 'completeness' in scholarship, promoting the embrace of 'incompleteness' as a catalyst for growth and collaboration. The address ultimately calls for a dynamic, decolonised approach to African scholarship that prioritises the continuous exchange of knowledge and mutual respect.

Introduction

This address expands on my keynote lecture, "Transforming African Scholarly Writing: Politics of Knowledge Production, Mobility and Conviviality",

---

[1] Updated from a Keynote address at the colloquium on 'Decolonising' knowledge production in the Humanities, Social Sciences and Arts (HSSA): Reflecting on a decade of the Charter for Humanities and Social Sciences in South African Higher Education 27-29 August 2024, Centre for Gender and Africa Studies, Faculty of the Humanities, University of The Free State, Bloemfontein; initially published by *Acta Academica* under the same title (DOI: https://doi.org/10.38140/aa.v56i2.8967, ISSN:0587-2405, e-ISSN: 2415-0479, *Acta Academica*, 2024 56(2): 198-222.

presented at the 2022 African Peacebuilding Network (APN) and Next Generation Fellows Virtual Writing and Dissemination Workshop.[2] I have made a slightly updated version of that lecture available for organisers of this colloquium to share with you.

For this conversation, I'd like to highlight Convivial Scholarship as a productive way to write and publish about Africa. Before sharing a story to anchor this discussion, let me briefly explain what I mean by this term.

Convivial Scholarship involves conversing and collaborating across disciplines and organisations, integrating knowledge from diverse sources, including popular understandings of reality. It recognises the importance of Indigenous and endogenous knowledge traditions that have been marginalised by colonial education and its exogenous prescriptive index. This approach acknowledges the inherent incompleteness of individuals, disciplines, and knowledge systems.

Please keep this concept in mind as we proceed. We'll revisit it in more detail after my story.

Collaboration for Transformation

When facing challenging situations, we often turn to oracles or those who can draw on the past and anticipate the future for guidance. One such figure, who has both lived as a human and transcended that form, can be found in the work of Amos Tutuola, a renowned archaeologist of African knowledge.

In his novel, *The Palm-Wine Drinkard*[3], Tutuola presents a character who embodies the concepts of incompleteness, mobility, and encounters – key

---

[2] The published version of that lecture is available at this link: https://www.ssrc.org/publications/transforming-african-scholarly-writing-politics-of-knowledge-production-mobility-and-conviviality/

[3] Tutuola, A. (1952), *The Palm-Wine Drinkard*, London: Faber and Faber

elements of Convivial Scholarship. This character is a skull, a relic of a once-human life.

This skull, though seemingly deactivated, still harbours human desires and ambitions. We encounter it through the story of the Palm-wine Drinkard, who has lost his beloved palm-wine tapster. The tapster, who skilfully harvested and served the wine, was essential to the Drinkard and his friends. Desperate to reunite with him, the Drinkard journeys to a town where the king is mourning the loss of his daughter.

The king's daughter was known for her lofty standards and expectations in a suitor. She systematically rejected numerous potential partners, much like a highly-rated journal that rejects many submissions.

This story, with its intriguing characters and themes, will help illustrate the concept of Convivial Scholarship and its relevance to African writing and publishing.

This skull, once a prominent human, understood human nature and how to manipulate it. Recognising humanity's obsession with appearances, the skull devised a plan to re-enter the world he knew so well.

Upon hearing of the king's daughter who rejected every suitor, the skull smiled, realising that a woman with such impossible standards must desire a husband from beyond the ordinary. He saw himself, reduced to a mere skull, as the perfect candidate.

However, the skull also understood the importance of appearances. He knew that approaching the princess in his current state would be futile. So, he embarked on a mission to borrow the best body parts available, like someone seeking to assemble the perfect physique.

This clever strategy highlights the skull's understanding of human vanity and his willingness to exploit it for his own gain.

Borrowing the finest body parts available, the skull transformed into what Amos Tutuola describes as "the complete gentleman." His appearance was so captivating that, were he in a war zone, one might hesitate to drop a bomb, fearing the destruction of such exquisite handsomeness. He was the epitome of perfection, akin to a flawless article or book written by an African scholar and published in a prestigious high impact journal or by a renowned book publisher in the Global North.

Upon seeing him, the king's daughter was instantly smitten, proclaiming him the one she had been waiting for. She readily agreed to follow him home, where a strange process of self-deactivation began. Not only was this gentleman impeccably handsome, but he was also a man of integrity, dedicated to fulfilling his obligations and repaying his debts.

This unexpected twist reveals the skull's true character, going beyond mere appearances to demonstrate a commitment to honour and responsibility.

Lessons from Tutuola

Amos Tutuola, who himself transitioned into the world of the skulls in 1997, uses the skull to teach us valuable life lessons. We, as incomplete beings, can only achieve our goals through the help of others. This activation comes through mobility, encounters, and collaboration – whether it's peer reviewers offering feedback, editors shaping our work, or a community of practice supporting our endeavours.

We are who we are because of those we encounter in our journeys. If we achieve success and then hoard the attributes that contribute to it, we deny others the opportunity to thrive. This desire for permanent completeness, where we refuse to repay our debts or help others succeed, ultimately hinders our own growth and the advancement of knowledge.

Let's imagine a scenario where the skull, after winning the princess, refuses to return the body parts he borrowed, claiming that his lenders are indebted to him instead. He would diminish and jeopardise those whose generosity had made success possible for him. He would jeopardise as well, the culture of being and becoming through others by living and letting live. This demonstrates the danger of seeking permanent completeness and the importance of acknowledging our debts to others.

Through the skull's story, Tutuola teaches us that success comes through encounters and collaborations, which inherently involve debt and indebtedness. No one should monopolise success or deny others the chance to achieve. Success for all is only possible through the circulation of opportunities, debt and indebtedness.

By using a skull – a figure who understands human desires for supremacy and completeness – Tutuola makes this message universally relatable. He reminds us of the African concept of Ubuntu, emphasising the importance of interconnectedness and becoming through relationships.

Tutuola also highlights the humility that should accompany scholarship and knowledge production. The skull's unravelling after achieving his goals serves as a reminder of the importance of recognising our debts and embracing the interconnectedness of knowledge creation. Every successful scholar, upon closer examination, is a composite – the product of encounters, debt and indebtedness.

This story teaches us that incompleteness doesn't have to be a weakness; it can be a catalyst for growth. We can activate our incompleteness through collaboration, mobility, and the exchange of knowledge. If we remain isolated, we become stagnant like the buried disembodied skull, only remembered as a relic of the past.

For scholars studying Africa, this message is particularly relevant. We must embrace the interconnectedness of knowledge and recognise that our work is not done in isolation. Our research, writing, and publishing are all part of a larger conversation, a continuous process of charging and discharging knowledge.

This process involves debt and indebtedness, where we borrow from and contribute to a shared pool of ideas. In this dynamic world, we should expect to encounter unexpected collaborators and conversation partners. Embracing this fluidity can lead to exciting new avenues of research and understanding.

This story reminds us that we can overcome our individual limitations by embracing collaboration and mobility. By engaging with scholars from diverse backgrounds and disciplines, we can enrich our research and create new knowledge.

We should expect to find African scholars in various parts of the world, and scholars from other regions working in Africa. This cross-pollination of ideas is essential for advancing knowledge production.

Compositeness as anchor in academic pursuits

I wanted to frame Convivial Scholarship in these terms to emphasise its innovative potential. It's not about dwelling on Africa's challenges or celebrating victimhood, but rather about actively engaging with diverse perspectives and forging meaningful collaborations. This approach allows us to move beyond simply diagnosing problems and towards creating solutions that empower African scholarship.

We can challenge academia to embrace incompleteness and reject the illusion of completeness. We should question the current template that prioritises a winner-takes-all approach to knowledge production. True completeness is unattainable, as it relies on denying our debts to others and ignoring the interconnected nature of knowledge as an ever unfolding conversation.

The story of the Skull teaches us about the importance of embracing our composite nature. Through mobility and encounters with strangers, we learn to take others in and become familiar with them. This process of internalising others allows us to export ourselves and our ideas into the world.

Ideas may originate in specific contexts, but through mobility and encounters with diverse perspectives, they evolve and adapt. Conversations, education, and cross-cultural experiences shape our understanding and contribute to the ongoing development of knowledge.

My personal journey, from the communal ethos of the Cameroon Grassfields to diverse corners of Africa and the world, has shaped a multifaceted identity. Like many, I've experienced varying degrees of mobility and the inherent incompleteness of human existence. Rather than creating a singular, linear self, these experiences have woven a tapestry of influences reflected in my scholarship.

Convivial Scholarship embraces this compositeness of being. It rejects singular identity markers and encourages us to embrace the complexity and nuance that arise from our diverse experiences and encounters.

In many ways, incomplete beings populate the world, each shaped by unique histories of mobility and encounters. Convivial Scholarship recognises this diversity and encourages us to challenge ourselves, move beyond fixed identities, and embrace the richness of our individual experiences.

This joy of encounters and interchanges is fundamental to Convivial Scholarship. I liken this process to the metaphor of a smartphone. While loaded with apps and capabilities, a smartphone is useless without a charge. In places with power outages, we suddenly realise how vital charging is.

A smartphone without power is like an unfulfilled promise, a window into a world of possibilities that remains inaccessible. It becomes deactivated, much like the skull that loses its borrowed body parts.

This metaphor highlights the importance of constant engagement and exchange in knowledge production. Just as a smartphone needs recharging to function, we need continuous interactions with others to fuel our intellectual growth.

When you recharge your phone's battery, it's just one form of activation. To fully utilise its capabilities, you need additional charges, such as airtime and data. Only then can you effectively communicate with others.

Once your phone is fully charged, interacting with others becomes a process of discharging. However, this discharging isn't a loss; it's a productive exchange. You share your resources – battery life, data, and airtime – through conversations, effectively charging up others. In turn, they discharge their knowledge and experiences, recharging you in the process.

This continuous exchange of knowledge and resources mirrors the dynamics of a scholarly community. We constantly interact with each other, sharing our research, insights, and perspectives. This exchange not only enriches our individual knowledge but also contributes to the collective advancement of scholarship.

This community of practice, this network of encounters, allows us to overcome our incompleteness and achieve our goals. We can claim success, not despite our imperfections, but because of them. By acknowledging our limitations and embracing collaboration, we open ourselves up to new possibilities.

Embracing incompleteness

To overcome the unequal power dynamics in academia, we need to shift our mindset. Instead of striving for supremacy, completeness, and perfection, we should embrace incompleteness as a universal truth. We need to foster horizontal encounters that prioritise collaboration and mutual respect over competition and dominance.

Like the skull who borrowed body parts to achieve his goal, we should be willing to share resources and knowledge, recognising that our success depends on the contributions of others. By embracing this mindset, we can create a more equitable and productive academic environment where everyone has the opportunity to thrive.

Imagine if the skull, after using Cristiano Ronaldo's, Lionel Messi's or Kylian Mbappe's leg to become a star footballer, refused to return it. Such ingratitude would be unimaginable! Similarly, in academia, we must acknowledge our debts to those who contribute to our success.

Convivial Scholarship emphasises humility and generosity of spirit. It encourages us to look beyond our disciplines, engage in interdisciplinary conversations, and listen to voices outside academia. It challenges the traditional ivory tower mentality and fosters a more inclusive approach to knowledge production.

This approach offers a hopeful message for African scholars. Instead of dwelling on victimhood narratives, we can focus on fostering collaboration, recognising our interdependencies, and building a more equitable and inclusive academic landscape.

With that, I'll open the floor for further discussion. Thank you.

Snippets of the discussion after the APN and Next Generation Fellows lecture

Question:

Francis, thank you for your fascinating perspective, using metaphors from literature, social science, and African wisdom to spark conversation and challenge existing paradigms. You've invited us to embrace connections rather than disconnections, and raised important questions about African scholarship: Who is an African scholar? How should they approach their work? What is the "right" way to reflect and write about Africa?

As the proverb says, "Many routes lead to the market." You've introduced the concept of Ubuntu scholarship, highlighting the importance of being through others. The question then becomes, how do we put this into practice as African scholars in our respective universities and contexts? How can we embrace interconnectedness and foster collaboration in our everyday work?

The metaphor of the skull borrowing body parts is indeed powerful. But how does this relate to a PhD student or a postdoctoral scholar in Africa? How can they apply this concept to their writing and career aspirations?

Yes, the skull had integrity and returned the borrowed parts. But what about the princess? How did she feel after discovering the truth? And who, in our everyday lives in Africa, represents the skull and the princess?

These are all intriguing questions, and I've raised them to stimulate further discussion.

Answer:

Those are excellent points. Let's revisit the skull metaphor and imagine a university student in Bamenda in the Cameroon Grassfields. The University of Bamenda is relatively new, and this student is immersed in the local scholarly context, using local resources and knowledge. They feel no need to explore beyond Bamenda because their current understanding seems sufficient.

However, this young scholar receives a call for participation in a conference in New York or Bloemfontein, sent by a sibling living abroad. This invitation challenges their assumptions about what constitutes valuable knowledge and opens up a new world of possibilities.

This call for participation challenges our Bamenda scholar to engage with unfamiliar scholarship and perspectives. They wonder how to compete successfully at this international level. They seek resources in a limited local library, reaching out to colleagues who may have participated in similar networks. Even then, they lack all the necessary elements.

They've already borrowed from their community, relying on those who understand the value of collaboration. However, if these colleagues subscribe to a competitive, zero-sum mindset, they may be hesitant to help, fearing that the student's success could threaten their own. This mentality of lone-ranger-ism has hindered African scholarship for far too long.

These colleagues, trapped in the mindset of individual success, may withhold their resources and connections. They view knowledge as a limited commodity, believing that sharing it diminishes their own advantage. This competitive model has severely hampered African scholarship.

Convivial Scholarship challenges this paradigm. It encourages generosity, sharing knowledge and networks freely. It recognises that scholarship thrives on collaboration and exchange, not isolation. Scholars are part of a community, engaging in ongoing conversations shaped by shared canons and ideas.

Our Bamenda student or colleague, seeking to participate in the New York or Bloemfontein conference, must navigate these challenges. They may see foreign or local conference and research funding or fellowships and grants as the ultimate prise, a validation of their individual achievement. But receiving the award is just the first step. They must then demonstrate their ability to engage with international scholarship, to participate in conversations and hold their own, not through arrogance or ambushing, but through humility and a willingness to exchange ideas.

Good scholarship is marked by curiosity, not by pretending to have all the answers. Isolation leads to stagnation, while engagement fosters growth and new discoveries.

In academia, as in life, no one is self-sufficient. We come to scholarship with questions, constantly seeking new angles to examine familiar topics. Chinua Achebe likened the world to a dancing masquerade, constantly in motion. Studying a dynamic continent like Africa requires us to move with it, exploring its ever-changing nimbleness, landscapes and perspectives.

This means examining the various social, cultural, and historical dimensions that shape African realities. We must consider class, ethnicity, race, gender, sexuality, and intergenerational dynamics along with how they intersect with one another to understand this complex phenomenon fully.

The scholar who borrows body parts from diverse sources, rather than relying on a single, predictable model, embodies the necessary nuance, complexity and open-endedness of a "complete gentleman" in motion. This approach is essential for engaging with the diverse and ever-evolving nature of African scholarship.

The skull metaphor is meant to be flexible, allowing you to substitute characters and contexts as you see fit. The princess's gullibility reminds us to look beyond appearances and superficial charm, grounding our ambitions in reality.

In the digital age, the skull's quest for completeness and self-enhancement would undoubtedly take on a new dimension, with access to a wealth of information and technologies that could aid in the pursuit of perfection.

A digital-era skull would not be limited to word-of-mouth accounts about the princess and her exacting standards. It would leverage the power of social media and dating apps to research her preferences and tailor its "enhancements" accordingly. If the princess were interested in reconciling gender binaries, the skull might borrow body parts from both men and women, blurring the lines of traditional gender roles. If she were passionate about climate change, the skull might incorporate elements from the natural world, reflecting her values and concerns. And if she wanted a humanoid, cyborg or something "half ghostly and half earthly" like a creature from Amos Tutuola's "My Life in the Bush of Ghosts", why would not the skull borrow accordingly?

This adaptation to the digital age highlights the fluidity of identity and the ever-evolving quest for self-improvement. The skull's actions would be a testament to the power of technology to shape our perceptions of self and the lengths we go to in order to fit in or stand out. It also underscores the importance of context in shaping our choices and the need to adapt to the changing landscape of social norms and values or, in scholarship, canons, prescriptions and expectations.

In essence, the digital era skull's quest for completeness would be a reflection of our own desires and anxieties in a world saturated with information and technology. It would be a story about the challenges and opportunities that come with the pursuit of self-improvement and distinction in a constantly evolving digital landscape.

Question:

The ideal of the "complete gentleman" is contextual, and enhancements ("*juju*") are borrowed and returned after use. What does stepping back from this ideal mean for the scholar? What does it mean to borrow new enhancements and become new versions of oneself in relation to Africa, the world, others, and one's own identity? In essence, what does the necessary fluctuation between completeness and incompleteness mean for a scholar?

Answer:

Completeness or incompleteness, when stagnant, starves us of productive encounters that generate opportunity and fulfilment. Humans, nature, and technology must constantly evolve. A scholar is always in motion, intellectually and otherwise. What is borrowed need not be returned, but circulated to extend fulfilment. An *entente cordiale* is necessary for all and sundry to maximise the benefits of such circulation. Privatisation, monopolisation, or immobilisation are dangerous, removing meaning from human pursuits and creating a false hierarchy between completeness and incompleteness.

Question:

Thank you, Francis, for your engaging lecture. I'd like to play devil's advocate here. You've eloquently described the importance of accommodating and internalising others, which seems to be a widespread practice in Africa. However, isn't this strategy prone to abuse if the parties involved don't approach the encounter with the same level of conviviality? Can one-sided conviviality exist? And what if, in your smartphone metaphor, the act of charging leads to complete depletion?

Answer:

That's an excellent question, and one I've been anticipating. Convivial Scholarship doesn't mean ignoring the existing power imbalances and inequalities within academia. It acknowledges the long history of violence and exclusion inherent in these structures.

The question is, how do we move beyond simply identifying these issues and instead create opportunities for those marginalised by these systems? How do we empower voices that have been silenced or disregarded?

I mentioned CODESRIA as an example of an organisation committed to challenging these hierarchies and fostering alternative knowledge production models. However, even CODESRIA faces limitations because it operates within the same system of zero-sum games and entrenched hierarchies. It's a painful reality, especially when the perpetrators of these inequalities are often members of the organisation itself.

I recall during my time at the CODESRIA secretariat in Dakar, we organised youth and gender institutes, issuing calls for participation similar to the hypothetical Bamenda scholar's foreign conference participation above. In CODESRIA's case, they diligently sent documentation to members, but these written materials often failed to represent the full breadth of their excellent scholarship. This suggests that even within African studies, African voices and perspectives can be overlooked or underrepresented.

It's a troubling realisation that one can easily ignore African scholarship and still be considered an expert in African studies. Even within the continent, scholars, like the Tutuola princess in her ambitions, may neglect the wealth of knowledge produced locally, focusing instead on external sources and perspectives.

I propose that we adopt Convivial Scholarship as a guiding principle, not apologetically, but as a challenge to the global academic community. This approach isn't exclusive to Africa; it's a call for everyone to engage in knowledge production differently.

We should challenge our colleagues at conferences and seminars, highlighting biases and skewed perspectives, as feminist scholars have done across various disciplines. Younger scholars are increasingly recognising the dominance of certain voices and demanding change.

Convivial Scholarship encourages diverse perspectives, challenging established norms, and promoting curiosity and intellectual growth. It refuses to let any discipline or individual rest on their laurels, assuming completeness based on power, authority or privilege.

So, I invite the devil, and all devil's advocates, to join this conversation and contribute to our understanding of Convivial Scholarship. Critical engagement is essential for meaningful progress.

Question[4]*:*

You've invited a devil's advocate perspective on Convivial Scholarship, so let me offer some critical challenges as obstacles to collaboration that highlight the tension between its ideals and the realities of the academic landscape, particularly for Africa-based scholars:

Unequal Resources and Infrastructure: Many Africa-based scholars face significant infrastructural hurdles that hinder their productivity and collaborative potential. While they may express willingness to participate, limited resources and support can make meaningful contributions and consistent engagement challenging.

Exploitation and Free-Riding: Convivial Scholarship, with its emphasis on shared knowledge and communal growth, can be vulnerable to exploitation. Some individuals may seek to gain knowledge and rewards without contributing meaningfully, potentially even pressuring collaborators to share research grants while remaining passive in the research itself. This breeds resentment and undermines the spirit of Ubuntu collaboration.

Competition and Mistrust: The academic environment, despite its emphasis on collaboration, often breeds intense competition and a scarcity mindset. This fosters a climate of mistrust where those who generously assist

---

[4] This question, not originally in the presentation, was a comment on the 2024 published version by my colleague at the University of Cape Town, Professor Asonzeh Ukah. It is hereby included with his permission.

others can become targets of envy and attack. A Yoruba proverb warns that a new king may eliminate the very person who helped them ascend to power. This "kill the kingmaker" mentality manifests in academia when supervisors and mentors find themselves accused of idea theft by their own mentees, eroding trust and undermining the very foundation of Convivial Scholarship.

Can Convivial Scholarship truly flourish within a system that seems designed to obstruct collaboration and perpetuate individualistic competition? I welcome your thoughts on this critique.

Answer:

My esteemed colleague, you raise valid concerns that strike at the core of Convivial Scholarship. These are not mere inconveniences, but significant obstacles that demand our attention if we truly seek to transform the academic landscape.

The issue of unequal resources and infrastructure is a pressing one. We cannot simply ignore the digital divide and the lack of support faced by many Africa-based scholars. Instead, we must become advocates for change. This means actively lobbying for increased funding and resource allocation, establishing mentorship networks to provide support and guidance, and fostering South-South collaborations to leverage existing strengths and resources.

The potential for exploitation and free-riding within Convivial Scholarship is a legitimate concern. To counter this, we must move beyond good intentions and establish clear collaboration agreements that outline each participant's roles, responsibilities, and expected contributions. Transparency and open communication are crucial. We must also be willing to address imbalances and ensure that the principle of reciprocity, so central to Ubuntu, is actively upheld.

And yes, the competitive nature of academia, with its pressure to publish and secure grants, can indeed create an environment where collaboration is hindered and mistrust festers. Instead of the "kingmaker paradox," perhaps we can draw upon the Xhosa proverb, "*umntu ngumntu ngabantu*" – "a person is a person through other people." This reminds us that our individual growth and success are inextricably linked to the well-being of the community. To foster this sense of interconnectedness, we must actively challenge the individualistic, "publish or perish" culture that dominates academia. We can do this by promoting collaborative research models, valuing mentorship and knowledge sharing, and celebrating collective achievements.

Convivial Scholarship transcends the narrative of victimhood; it champions agency and transformation. It acknowledges challenges, not as insurmountable barriers, but as opportunities for growth and collective empowerment. It recognises our interconnectedness, striving to build a more equitable and inclusive academic space where knowledge is truly shared and celebrated.

Let us not shy away from these complexities, but embrace them in the spirit of Ubuntu. Through collective effort and mutual support, we can create a symphony of knowledge that resonates far beyond the walls of academia. Ubuntu reminds us that our destinies are intertwined – we either succeed together, or perish together. A civilisation that solely prioritises success, neglecting the lessons of failure, is ultimately unsustainable. True progress requires embracing both optimism and pessimism, recognising that they are two sides of the same coin, essential for navigating the complexities of life.

Question:

Thank you, Professor Nyamnjoh, for your insightful talk. I have two questions:

Some mentors encourage us to share our work, even in its incomplete form, to foster conversation and generosity. However, there seem to be two extremes when it comes to incompleteness. On one hand, oversharing can lead to being overwhelmed by others' ideas and losing our own voice. On the other extreme, isolation can lead to feelings of completeness or imposter syndrome. How do you navigate these extremes?

Often, ideas are viewed as competitive rather than complementary. We strive for the "best" ideas instead of collaborating and contributing different perspectives. How can we foster a Convivial Scholarship that emphasises collaboration and complementarity over competition?

You've raised a crucial point about balancing individual expression and collaboration. In the first half of Tutuola's story, the skull seeks to stand out by borrowing the "best" body parts, driven by a competitive desire. However, real-life encounters are often less deliberate, and the knowledge we gain from them isn't always immediately applicable. It's when faced with a challenge that we sift through our diverse experiences and find unexpected solutions.

Answer:

Convivial Scholarship embraces this organic process, blurring the lines between academic and everyday knowledge, just as it blurs disciplinary boundaries. It doesn't negate specialisation but encourages us to draw inspiration from diverse sources and engage in cross-disciplinary conversations.

There's always a point of origin. In the written version of this keynote address, I argue that we've overused the term "international," assuming certain locations are inherently superior. But even a child born in Oxford or Cambridge starts their intellectual journey in a local context. They learn about the global significance of institutions such as Oxford and Cambridge universities later on.

Your question about generosity with scholarship highlights another problem. We're often trained to hoard our ideas, fearing that sharing them diminishes our value. We must not shy away from sharing, even when the danger is real of others not just borrowing, but even stealing ideas and presenting them as their own. This mindset reinforces a singular, fixed identity based on individual ownership of knowledge.

However, if we truly recognised the absence of a unified self, we would embrace the potential of our incompleteness. We find life and fulfilment through mobility and encounters that continuously shape and reshape us as composite beings.

We are all a patchwork of experiences, starting with our families. Even before birth, we're connected to the outside world through the umbilical cord. Life is a constant process of coming to terms with our incompleteness, not as a weakness, but as a fundamental aspect of existence.

By celebrating incompleteness and mobility, we can approach scholarship as a conversation, not a monologue. We don't need to overwhelm others with our knowledge but can instead engage in a mutual exchange of ideas, acknowledging our individual strengths and weaknesses.

Convivial Scholarship encourages us to reject the notion of permanent completeness. It's pointless to hoard knowledge like a fully charged smartphone that never gets used. We are energised by the conversations and kindred fulfilment that an energised or charged smartphone brings our way. The purpose of knowledge is to be shared, to spark conversations, and to create new understanding.

Question:

Thank you, Professor Nyamnjoh. Your presentation on conviviality reminded me of your paper on the elephant and the blind men at the 2012 Anthropology Southern Africa conference. It beautifully illustrates how different perspectives shape our understanding, much like the blind men feeling various parts of the elephant.

In the context of Convivial Scholarship and writing, could you elaborate on how this metaphor applies? Specifically, how does it relate to knowledge production in Africa?

Additionally, I'm intrigued by your concept of resistance to colonial education. How does this resistance interact with the idea of convivial writing? What implications does it hold for young, emerging African scholars?

Answer:

Thank you for your question and for recalling my presentation on the elephant and the blind men. That metaphor indeed aligns with the concept of Convivial Scholarship, where diverse perspectives contribute to a richer understanding of complex subjects.

To juxtapose the two, the elephant metaphor illustrates the limitations of individual perspectives. Each blind man, touching a different part of the elephant, forms a partial understanding. Only by combining their experiences can they grasp the whole picture.

Similarly, Convivial Scholarship acknowledges that no single discipline or individual holds the complete truth. It encourages collaboration and the integration of diverse viewpoints to create a richer, more nuanced understanding of Africa.

Regarding your second point about resisting colonial education while embracing convivial writing, I believe these two concepts can coexist. Convivial Scholarship challenges the dominance of Western knowledge systems while valuing and incorporating Indigenous African knowledge traditions. It's about recognising the plurality of knowledge and creating space for diverse voices and perspectives.

For young and emerging scholars, this approach is particularly empowering. It allows them to draw on their unique experiences and cultural backgrounds, challenging established norms and contributing to a more inclusive and representative body of African scholarship.

To dwell a little further on the elephant and the blind men, let me share another metaphor from Cameroon. In the forest regions, they say that cooking an elephant is no easy feat; it requires immense effort and patience. It's a task that cannot be rushed.

Similarly, understanding knowledge, like understanding an elephant, requires time and ongoing interaction. The blind men in the story realised that their individual perspectives were limited, but by sharing their experiences, they could collectively gain a more complete understanding.

This metaphor highlights the importance of patience and collaboration in knowledge production. We shouldn't rush to conclusions or assume that our individual perspectives are all-encompassing. Instead, we should engage in ongoing conversations and exchange ideas to deepen our understanding.

Knowledge acquisition is a continuous process. As you progress through your studies, you start with a narrow focus, which gradually expands as you delve deeper. This can be overwhelming, so it's crucial to reframe and narrow your focus to make a meaningful contribution to your field. This doesn't mean oversimplifying complex issues, but rather focusing on a specific area to contribute to the larger conversation.

The story of the blind men and the elephant illustrates that partial knowledge is inevitable, even within a specific discipline. We all have limited perspectives, and it's through sharing and collaboration that we can gain a more comprehensive understanding.

Even the elephant itself might struggle to fully comprehend its own complexity. It relies on experts, like veterinarians and medical practitioners, to analyse and explain its anatomy. This highlights the importance of interdisciplinary collaboration in knowledge production. No single perspective is complete, and we all benefit from sharing our knowledge and expertise.

Being part of something doesn't equate to complete self-knowledge. The elephant, while inherently "elephant," may not fully grasp its own nature. Others, observing from different angles, might offer valuable insights. This relates to the dancing masquerade metaphor – studying a dynamic, ever-changing phenomenon like Africa requires examining it from multiple perspectives.

When conducting research, clearly define and situate your audience. Different disciplines approach phenomena differently; a geographer's perspective will differ from a sociologist's or a political scientist's. We often define a phenomenon first, then explore it through our disciplinary lens.

We must avoid hasty claims to knowledge and acknowledge the validity of diverse perspectives. As Chinua Achebe wisely noted, each generation must forge its own artistic path, building upon or challenging the achievements of its predecessors. This principle extends to scholarship as well. Our understanding of Africa has evolved since CODESRIA's founding in 1973. Africans have traversed borders, bringing varied experiences and perspectives, with diasporic Africans and their children playing prominent roles in CODESRIA, navigating complex identity landscapes.

To remain relevant, we must keep pace with this evolving reality. Conviviality, as I define it, acknowledges incompleteness and embraces mobility and encounters. This differs from other interpretations of conviviality, which assume completeness.

My understanding of conviviality is rooted in the recognition of our composite nature. When we embrace our incompleteness and engage with others, we create opportunities for growth, collaboration, and new knowledge production.

The skull, living with borrowed body parts, had to choreograph them to function as a unified whole, not a disjointed mess. Similarly, Convivial Scholarship involves harmonising the diverse knowledge and experiences we acquire through encounters and mobility. It's about integrating these disparate elements into a coherent and effective approach to our work.

Imagine an African scholar whose journey begins in a village or city, then moves through Afropolitan and cosmopolitan spaces, eventually landing at a prestigious university like Stanford, Harvard, Penn State, Columbia or Toronto. Each of these experiences contributes to their unique perspective, creating a scholar who defies easy categorisation.

Convivial Scholarship encourages us to embrace this complexity. We don't have to shed our diverse experiences and perspectives to conform to a single narrative. Instead, we can bring our full selves to our scholarship, acknowledging the richness and nuance that arises from our journeys.

In today's digital age, our capacity to access and store vast amounts of knowledge is akin to carrying a terabyte hard drive. This wealth of information allows us to draw from diverse sources and perspectives, enriching our understanding and fostering a more inclusive and dynamic approach to knowledge production. We should emulate ChatGPT's effortless navigation of information networks, even as we maintain a critical eye towards its limitations.

Question:

Conviviality and Networking: How can we apply the philosophy of conviviality to networking and building collaborations among African scholars, both within the continent and in the diaspora? How can we create networks that facilitate the exchange of knowledge, resources, and opportunities?

Publishing in Africa: There's a common perception that international publishers hold a monopoly on academic publishing and often disadvantage African scholars and perspectives. Given your experience in publishing in Africa, can you share your insights on how to access reputable, internationally competitive Africa-based publishing outlets?

Answer:

Regarding publishing on the continent, CODESRIA stands as a shining example. They've achieved remarkable milestones, unmatched by any other publisher in Africa. Others have followed suit, making significant strides in their own right. I've personally served on the boards of HSRC Press and Langaa, working alongside the African Books Collective, which CODESRIA co-founded.

Together, we've made African scholarship accessible and competitive, even in spaces where it was once dismissed or overlooked. Students can no longer claim that African scholarship is absent from libraries or irrelevant to their studies.

African scholarship is readily available if you know where to look. Various scholarly networks on the continent and in the diaspora can play a crucial role in promoting this scholarship by sharing resources, connecting scholars, and highlighting relevant research. This includes sharing electronic books, journal articles, and contact information for experts in various fields. And, given the growing popularity of social media, we could harness platforms such as TikTok, Instagram, Facebook and X to share snippets about publications in addition to what Academia Edu and ResearchGate make available. I once read a full insightful review of my book, *Drinking from the Cosmic Gourd: How Amos Tutuola Can Change Our Minds*[5], which was ventilated entirely on X by Professor Grace Musila of the University of the Witwatersrand.

---

[5] Nyamnjoh, F. B. (2017) *Drinking from the Cosmic Gourd: How Amos Tutuola Can Change Our Minds*, Bamenda: Langaa.

The networks we create and sustain with our scholarly generosity can be used effectively to enhance scholarship and foster collaboration, without relying solely on external sources or perpetuating the notion of African scholars as perpetual pupils.

I'm glad you find the concept of Convivial Scholarship productive. It's a vast topic with many avenues for exploration.

If decolonisation truly values Indigenous African languages and their diverse speakers, the publishing industry still has a long way to go. Despite progress, Indigenous language works continue to face systemic barriers, including geographic biases and the dominance of prestige languages. Henry Chakava, a prominent figure in East African publishing, identified these challenges as early as 1977, noting linguistic variations, lack of standardised orthography, and the limited pool of authors, editors, and readers for specific languages.[6]

Chakava's passing in 2024 raises the question: has the landscape of African language publishing significantly changed since his observations? Despite a surge in decolonial scholarship, the reality often falls short of the rhetoric. Even with standardised orthography and technical advancements, Indigenous language publishing has not flourished. South Africa's Lovedale Press, established in 1823, serves as a prime example of this enduring struggle. The gap between theory and practice remains a critical issue in decolonising African literature and scholarship.

Lovedale was a pioneer in publishing African literature, particularly in isiXhosa. It provided a platform for Black authors and trained Black South Africans in printing and bookbinding. Despite its historical significance, marked by a plaque with a quote

---

[6] Chakava, H. (1977) "Publishing in a Multilingual Situation: the Kenya Case", *The African Book Publishing Record*, UNESCO. Pp.83-90.

from renowned Xhosa author AC Jordan –"The earliest record of anything written by any Bantu-speaking African in his own language in South Africa was made at the small printing press at Old Lovedale." –, Lovedale faced bankruptcy and ceased publishing in 2015. Efforts are now underway to revive Lovedale Press, led by the Thabo Mbeki Foundation in collaboration with several universities.[7] I would suggest these consultations be done in conversation with AI. This potential revival could revitalise Lovedale's legacy in education, religion, culture, and literature, as seen through the contributions of Black South African authors, printers, and bookbinders. Decolonisation of scholarship on the continent should provide for developing and sustaining scholarly publishing on the continent, with scholars who clamour for decolonisation taking leadership in supporting publishers on the continent.

Question:

What is the difference between Convivial Scholarship and decoloniality?

Answer:

To answer your question, let me address the distinction between conviviality and decoloniality. While both approaches aim to challenge power imbalances and create more inclusive knowledge systems, they differ in their emphasis and strategies.

Decoloniality primarily focuses on dismantling colonial structures and legacies, particularly in knowledge production. It critiques the dominance of

---

[7] Sandiso Phaliso, "Reviving history: Thabo Mbeki Foundation aims to restore Eastern Cape's 200-year-old Lovedale Press", https://www.news24.com/life/books/reviving-history-thabo-mbeki-foundation-aims-to-restore-eastern-capes-200-year-old-lovedale-press-20240606, accessed 07 June 2024.

Western epistemologies and advocates for centring marginalised voices and perspectives.

Conviviality, on the other hand, emphasises collaboration, exchange, and the recognition of interconnectedness. It seeks to create a more equitable and inclusive academic environment by fostering dialogue and mutual respect among diverse scholars and knowledge systems.

While decoloniality is essential for dismantling oppressive structures, conviviality offers a way to move beyond critique and towards building new, more inclusive forms of knowledge production. It avoids the pitfalls of appropriation by emphasising collaboration and mutual respect, rather than simply replacing one dominant narrative with another.

I believe Convivial Scholarship can complement decolonial efforts by fostering dialogue and collaboration between scholars from diverse backgrounds, creating a space where multiple perspectives can coexist and enrich each other.

Decoloniality, when pursued within a framework of zero-sum victories, seeks to undo colonial violence and violations through complete rupture and unravelling. It's a radical approach, akin to the skull's complete deactivation or complete activation in Tutuola's story.

It is true that humans are wired for a sense of completeness, even if fleeting. We often cling to notions of ownership and control, which can hinder true decolonisation. This is where Convivial Scholarship offers an alternative. It acknowledges the interconnectedness of knowledge and encourages collaboration and exchange rather than complete separation.

While decoloniality aims to reclaim and restore what was lost, Convivial Scholarship focuses on building new, more inclusive knowledge systems. It recognises that knowledge is not a fixed entity but a dynamic process shaped by diverse perspectives and experiences.

Indeed, complete decolonisation might require a radical rupture, like the skull's unravelling. But it's a complex process. Can we truly undo the colonial education that shaped us, even after achieving a PhD in coloniality? Perhaps decolonisation is about acknowledging and embracing our inherent incompleteness, mobility, encounters, and composite nature. It's about recognising our debts and engaging in convivial knowledge production. This notion is in itself subversive in relation to many traditional or conventional dominant narratives from the Global North.

This approach offers a nuanced understanding of decolonisation, moving beyond simple reversals of power, authority and privilege. Incompleteness becomes a framework for continuous growth and collaboration, rather than a static state of achieved liberation.

Consider the landmark publication *Engendering African Social Sciences*[8], which emerged after CODESRIA's significant contributions. It highlighted the dominance of male voices and perspectives in African scholarship, even within a decolonial framework. This demonstrates that even successful decolonial efforts can be incomplete, requiring further critique and engagement. This is an example of the necessity of having an intersectional perspective. Otherwise, doubly and triply marginalised perspectives, narratives and representations risk being re-marginalised even within progressive movements.

Just as a perspective is never complete, so too is the work of decolonising knowledge. CODESRIA's success in establishing an African perspective was significant, but it's an ongoing process. The initial focus on gender has expanded to include youth, children, language, sexuality and more. This demonstrates the

---

[8] Imam A, Mama A and Sow F (eds) (1997) *Engendering African Social Sciences*. Dakar: CODESRIA.

evolving nature of knowledge production and the need for continuous reassessment and inclusion.

If we cling to the notion of completeness, we become defensive when faced with critiques or calls for change. Instead, we should embrace the idea that knowledge is a perpetual work in progress. By acknowledging our limitations – including missteps and errors, accepting these and using them as learning opportunities rather than seeing them as something shameful or anathema – and welcoming new perspectives, we can foster a more dynamic and inclusive academic landscape.

This applies to individual scholars as well. We should strive to be perpetual questioners, constantly seeking new knowledge and challenging our own assumptions.

Question:

What tips do you have for overcoming challenges in writing?

Answer:

To answer your question about overcoming challenges in writing, I've certainly faced moments of doubt and frustration in my own journey. What motivates me during those times is a deep-seated belief in the importance of my work. I remind myself of the potential impact my research can have on people's lives and the broader understanding of African realities.

For colleagues facing similar challenges, I offer this advice:

Remember your purpose: Why did you start writing in the first place? What are you passionate about? Reconnect with your purpose and the potential impact of your work.

Embrace the process: Writing is a journey, not a destination. There will be setbacks and challenges along the way. Focus on the process of learning and discovery, rather than the end product.

Seek support: Don't isolate yourself. Reach out to colleagues, mentors, or writing groups for guidance and encouragement. Share your work with trusted peers and welcome their feedback.

Take breaks: Step away from your work when you feel stuck. Engage in activities that inspire you and recharge your creative energy.

Celebrate small victories: Acknowledge your progress and celebrate small milestones along the way. This will help you stay motivated and build confidence in your abilities.

Overcoming challenges in writing often requires unconventional approaches and finding inspiration from unexpected sources. Sometimes, seeking feedback from peers or even those unfamiliar with your topic can offer fresh perspectives.

Inspiration can come from anywhere – music, nature, conversations, sleep. Personally, when I need to write about Africa, I listen to Fela Kuti's music at high volume. It puts me in a daring mood, ready to tackle any obstacle.

I encourage you to explore different techniques and find what works best for you. However, it's crucial to share your work with trusted individuals. Not everyone will offer constructive feedback or have your best interests at heart.

It's important to be discerning about who you share your work with. As I have already admitted above, there's a risk of having your ideas prematurely appropriated or misrepresented, especially in the age of social media. It's crucial to trust your instincts and share your work with those who will offer constructive feedback and support.

There's no single formula for overcoming writer's block or maintaining motivation. Different approaches work for different people. Sometimes, seeking inspiration from peers or engaging in unrelated activities can help. I find that working on multiple projects simultaneously can be beneficial. If I get stuck on one piece, I can switch to another, and sometimes, the act of switching can spark new ideas.

Teaching can also be a source of inspiration. Lightbulb moments often occur during classroom discussions, leading to new insights and research directions.

Ultimately, it's about finding what works for you and trusting the process. Remember, writing is a journey, not a destination. Embrace the challenges and celebrate the small victories along the way.

Question:

How do we keep researching in contexts of dwindling research funding?

Answer:

We need to explore alternative funding sources. We could encourage our billionaires, like Dangote and Motsepe, to invest in research, perhaps by endowing positions at CODESRIA or universities. We already offer them honorary degrees for a fee; perhaps we can leverage that to secure research funding.

We could also approach our footballers, suggesting they invest their wealth in research instead of luxury cars. There's a wealth of potential for exciting research on football in Africa, as I saw during my visit to Amsterdam, where scholars were actively studying the sport. We could replicate those efforts here in our universities.

Yes, funding often comes with strings attached. But many researchers have learned to navigate these constraints, going beyond the narrow terms set by donors to explore broader theoretical possibilities. It's about finding ways to satisfy both the funder's requirements and our own intellectual pursuits. We can "shoot two birds with one stone," even when dealing with those who seek to control rather than enable.

Conclusion

In closing, our vibrant dialogue today has illuminated the transformative power of Convivial Scholarship[9]. The metaphors and symbols we've explored – the skull's strategic borrowing, the smartphone's charge and discharge, the elephant's multifaceted nature – weave a rich tapestry for future scholarly conversations about the dynamic landscape of African knowledge production.

As you continue your academic journeys, I urge you to embrace the essence of Convivial Scholarship. Let collaboration, interconnectedness, and the celebration of diverse perspectives guide your research and writing. Remember that knowledge is not a solitary pursuit but a collective endeavour, fuelled by the continuous exchange of ideas and experiences.

As you embark on this journey, consider these guiding questions:

Contextualising Convivial Scholarship: How can you tailor the principles of Convivial Scholarship to your specific academic environment? What unique opportunities and challenges does your context present for fostering collaboration, interdisciplinarity, and the integration of diverse knowledge sources?

Navigating Challenges: The pursuit of Convivial Scholarship, while transformative, is not without its hurdles. The allure of 'completeness', deeply ingrained in traditional academic structures, can create resistance to the embrace of incompleteness and collaboration. Power dynamics and entrenched hierarchies may pose challenges to fostering a truly inclusive and equitable environment for knowledge production. What

---

[9] Nyamnjoh, F.B. (2020) *Decolonising the Academy: A Case for Convivial Scholarship* (Carl Schlettwein Lecture 14), Basel: Basler Afrika; Nyamnjoh, F.B. (2019) "Decolonizing the University in Africa," *Oxford Research Encyclopedias*, Oxford University Press, DOI: 10.1093/acrefore/9780190228637.013.717, pp.1-36.

challenges and limitations might you encounter in implementing this approach? How can you proactively address these challenges and ensure the success of your collaborative endeavours?

Balancing Collaboration and Individuality: The pursuit of knowledge often involves a delicate balance between collaboration and individual recognition. How can you navigate this tension within the framework of Convivial Scholarship? How can you ensure that your contributions are acknowledged and valued while fostering a spirit of shared ownership and collective achievement?

By actively engaging with these questions and incorporating Convivial Scholarship into your practices, you have the power to shape a more inclusive, dynamic, and impactful scholarly landscape in Africa. The journey towards decolonised knowledge production is ongoing, requiring our collective commitment. It begins with each of us embracing our incompleteness and recognising the transformative potential of collaboration and mobility.

Victoria Ogoegbunam Okoye's thoughtful response, in an email to me on September 20, 2024 (here included with her permission), to this keynote beautifully captures the essence of Convivial Scholarship and its potential to inspire and guide us on this journey:

> Dear Francis,
>
> Thank you for sharing your insightful talk on Convivial Scholarship. Your emphasis on embracing incompleteness and fostering collaboration resonates deeply with my current academic context.
>
> Your exploration of the skull's strategic borrowing of body parts highlights the importance of intentional relationship-building in scholarly pursuits. It prompts us to consider not only how we collaborate but also with whom we choose to engage. Your thoughtful responses to questions about the challenges and complexities of

embodying conviviality offer valuable guidance as we navigate the inevitable trials and errors on this path.

Your redefinition of indebtedness, shifting it away from its capitalist connotations, is particularly illuminating. It underscores the generative potential of acknowledging our interconnectedness and recognising that scholarly ideas are shaped by a multitude of influences. Your talk encourages a more transparent and honest approach to knowledge production, acknowledging the contributions of others and fostering a culture of care within academia.

Your work is particularly relevant to my current position at a Scottish university housed in a building with historical ties to Caribbean enslavement. Your insights on conviviality and incompleteness have prompted me to reflect on the necessary humility, transparency, and care required to honour the complex histories and debts associated with this space. I am inspired to continue grappling with these ideas and their implications for my scholarship and engagement within this context.

Thank you again for your generosity in sharing your work and for your kind words about mine. I look forward to staying connected and continuing this enriching conversation.

Warm regards,
Victoria

Victoria Ogoegbunam Okoye's words remind us that Convivial Scholarship is not merely an abstract concept, but a powerful tool for addressing the complexities and injustices of our world. By embracing collaboration, acknowledging our interconnectedness, and fostering a culture of care, we can create a more just and equitable academic landscape that honours the diverse histories and perspectives that shape our knowledge production.

Let us all be inspired by Victoria Ogoegbunam Okoye's reflections and commit to fostering a scholarly environment where diverse voices are heard, knowledge is shared generously, and collaboration is celebrated. The future of African scholarship is bright, and together, we can create a more inclusive, dynamic, and impactful landscape for generations to come.

Part III
Celebrating Pioneers: Indigenous Publishing and the Legacy of Henry Chakava

Henry Miyinzi Chakava: A Pioneer of Indigenous Publishing in Kenya and Africa[1]

Abstract

This article pays tribute to Henry Chakava, a pioneering figure who played a pivotal role in transforming African publishing. It examines his significant contributions to promoting indigenous publishing, supporting African languages, and facilitating translation, while also addressing the challenges he faced, including the dominance of multinational corporations and the complexities of fostering a sustainable publishing ecosystem in Africa. The article explores Chakava's lasting legacy and its impact on the African literary landscape, considering the future of African publishing and drawing inspiration from his work to address ongoing challenges and promote diverse African narratives in the face of globalisation.

Introduction

Henry Miyinzi Chakava, born on April 26, 1946, in Vokoli village, Vihiga County, Kenya, was a visionary and indefatigable force in African publishing. Revered as the 'father of Kenyan publishing' since 1972 – "the year UNESCO designated as International Book Year", he was also described by his Tanzanian contemporary, publisher Walter Bgoya, as 'the publisher who pricked

[1] I am most grateful to Kiarie Kamau, Chief Executive Officer, East African Educational Publishers Limited, for comments and suggestions on a draft paper that have inspired this tribute.

the people into consciousness…best remembered for publishing some of the giants of East African literature – Okot p'Bitek, Mazrui, Meja Mwangi, Marjorie Oludhe-Macgoye, and most notably (and riskily), Ngugi wa Thiong'o' (Bgoya 2016)[2]. This Nairobi-based "indefatigable" "colossus" of a publisher and "visionary who confronts change and challenge with admirable flexibility" dedicated his life to shaping the continent's literary landscape (Kamau 2016: 13). Beyond his commercial achievements, Chakava championed African languages, facilitated crucial translation efforts, and challenged the dominance of multinational publishers. His passing on March 8, 2024, after nearly fifty years of tireless work, leaves a profound void. This tribute illuminates Chakava's enduring legacy, examining his pivotal initiatives and their lasting impact on the Kenyan and African publishing world.

Challenging Multinational Control

Chakava also challenged the dominance of multinational publishers and the perpetuation of colonial narratives in Kenya (Chakava 1988), narratives which often continued even when the authors were local, as African writers were often reduced to the palatability indicators of their European publishers (Nyamnjoh 2004). According to his lecturer, author and friend since 1969, Taban Lo Liyong, Chakava, who graduated with first-class honours in BA Literature, 'was lured by Professor Simeon Ominde [as well as Professor Andrew Gurr (Kamau 2016: 2-3)] to join

[2] Walter Bgoya, "Henry Chakava (1946 – 2024): The publisher who pricked the people into consciousness", https://africanarguments.org/2024/04/henry-chakava-the-publisher-who-pricked-the-people-into-consciousness/, accessed March 19, 2025.

Heinemann as an apprentice publisher'[3], where he worked with Bob Markham whom he later succeeded as managing director at the age of 30 (Currey 2008: xviii). In a groundbreaking move, he spearheaded the acquisition of Heinemann Educational Books East Africa Ltd (later Heinemann Kenya, now East African Educational Publishers), the first instance of a local publisher taking over a multinational publishing house in the country[4]. The 1992 rebranding to East African Educational Publishers (EAEP) signified a pivotal shift. He transformed the company from a conduit for manuscripts sent to London for evaluation and publication, to a fully-fledged local publishing house, thereby significantly impacting the Kenyan industry (Currey 2016; Jay 2016: 203-204).This bold move had a ripple effect, paving the way for other local publishers to acquire established multinational companies, such as Longman and Macmillan[5]. These acquisitions significantly altered the Kenyan publishing landscape, empowering local voices and fostering a more diverse and representative literary environment (Kamau 2016:4-6). As Bgoya remarks, "From being 'a representative of a filthy multinational' Henry became a pioneer in the indigenisation of foreign publishing

---

[3] Taban Lo Liyong, "An elegy to my student and publisher Henry Chakava," https://nation.africa/kenya/life-and-style/weekend/taban-lo-liyong-an-elegy-to-my-student-and-publisher-henry-chakava-4565572, accessed March 19, 2025.

[4] Chakava, Henry, "Publishing Ngugi: The Challenge, the Risk and the Reward." *African Publishing Review* 3, no. 4 (July/August 1994): 10-14; see also Dr Henry Chakava: Father of Kenyan publishing takes final bow - The Standard, accessed March 12, 2025, https://www.standardmedia.co.ke/national/article/2001491124/dr-henry-chakava-father-of-kenyan-publishing-takes-final-bow

[5] Dr Henry Chakava: Father of Kenyan publishing takes final bow - The Standard, accessed March 12, 2025, https://www.standardmedia.co.ke/national/article/2001491124/dr-henry-chakava-father-of-kenyan-publishing-takes-final-bow

companies providing a how-to model." (Bgoya 2016: ix).

This shift in ownership, however, presented challenges for the remaining multinational publishers, such as Oxford University Press. They faced increased competition from local publishers who were more attuned to the needs and preferences of the Kenyan market[6]. Furthermore, these multinational publishers had to contend with issues like piracy and distribution barriers, which significantly impacted their operations and market share[7]. The rise of local publishing houses forced them to adapt their strategies to remain relevant in the evolving landscape.

Writers face administrative censorship or high rejection rates from commercial multinational publishers. However, African publishers, through remarkable resilience and commitment, have brought to light books that would otherwise have remained unpublished, though printing and binding quality often leaves much to be desired. As Chakava highlighted in his introduction to Hans Zell's 2008 *Publishing, Books & Reading in Sub-Saharan Africa: A Critical Bibliography*, many African writers, from novelists to academics, poets, playwrights, and journalists, seek visibility through publication, yet their efforts often perish, not necessarily due to poor content (Chakava 2008). Rather, publishers often lack the capacity to ensure quality and effectively disseminate their publications. This results in a situation where publishing is reduced to simply producing a book and expecting it to sell itself, or, as Chakava puts it, to "light a lamp and hide

---

6 The Role of Publishing Companies in Kenya, accessed March 12, 2025, https://iread.ke/the-role-of-publishing-companies-in-kenya/

7 The Role of Publishing Companies in Kenya, accessed March 12, 2025, https://iread.ke/the-role-of-publishing-companies-in-kenya/

it under a bushel" (Bgoya 2016:x)[8] These challenges are particularly acute for those writing and attempting to publish in indigenous African languages.

In the social sciences, African scholars navigate a precarious tightrope, caught between the desire for global recognition and the imperative of local relevance. The cultural economy of publishing often forces a painful choice: sacrifice one for the other. This dilemma is particularly acute when Africa suffers a critical famine – a famine of books rooted in its own diverse cultures. Deprived of their intellectual nourishment, communities struggle to cultivate confidence and agency (Nyamnjoh 2004; Mlambo 2007).

As with any famine, well-intentioned aid and opportunistic exploitation are never far behind. A surge of external "do-gooders" has descended, promising to alleviate this cultural poverty by flooding the continent with books. However, these well-meaning efforts often mask a deeper problem: a disregard for African perspectives and needs, as defined by Africans themselves. Many of these imported texts, laden with unexamined assumptions and a lingering colonial gaze, serve to undermine, rather than uplift, African self-worth. In essence, much of this book donation becomes a form of cultural and intellectual dumping, a deluge of pre-packaged ideas from Europe and North America, with little regard for fostering genuine cultural diversity.

Even those who recognise the potential benefits of thoughtfully tailored book donations criticise the lack of strategic vision in these endeavours. Hans Zell, a leading advocate for African publishing, decries the continued reliance on externally driven initiatives,

---

[8] Walter Bgoya, "Henry Chakava (1946 – 2024): The publisher who pricked the people into consciousness", https://africanarguments.org/2024/04/henry-chakava-the-publisher-who-pricked-the-people-into-consciousness/, accessed March 19, 2025.

emphasising the urgent need to build indigenous capacity. Why, after decades of independence and the tireless efforts of champions like Henry Chakava, do African libraries remain dependent on foreign book donations? This reliance raises fundamental questions about the sustainability and autonomy of African intellectual production, and underscores the ongoing struggle to reclaim and redefine the narrative of the continent. Zell is right to worry if anyone is genuinely interested in an independent African library when, in 2015, he writes:

> … I believe legitimate to ask why large scale book donation programmes should continue to be necessary today, after millions of books have been shipped and donated to African libraries, schools and other recipients every year, and over the last three decades or more. Just when can we expect African libraries to become independent of large scale foreign book aid and create their own sustainable library services? (Zell 2015: 43)

The persistent exclusion of African-published books from donation programs remains a concern, as confirmed by commissioned studies (Gray et al. 2010), even though the African Books Collective effectively markets and distributes over 200 new titles each year from 155 publishers across 24 African countries (Jay 2016: 216).[9] The continued disregard for locally published African books by donation programs is deeply perplexing, especially given the World Bank's own findings. Their report (Fredriksen et al. 2015: 33) unequivocally states that locally produced books are the most cost-effective and culturally appropriate, and that Africa possesses the capacity to populate its reading landscape with relevant, indigenous publications. What, then, fuels this persistent resistance? Why do donors consistently overlook the potential for valuable

---

[9] See http://www.africanbookscollective.com/about-us, accessed 01 February 2016.

contributions from Africa, perpetuating a narrative of dependency and dominance? Why is there an a priori assumption that African content is either non-existent or inaccessible? This bias directly undermines local publishers and stifles the growth of African publishing.

The irony is that the necessary distribution solutions, particularly with the rise of electronic publishing, are readily available. What remains absent are the crucial financial investments. This regression is particularly disheartening when compared to the era of Henry Chakava's influence. During that period, initiatives like the Intra-African Book Support Scheme (IABSS), which operated from 1991 to 2004, fostered significant co-publication partnerships between African and international publishers, demonstrating the potential for collaborative and sustainable growth (Jay 2016: 211). The current reluctance to support local publishing, despite clear evidence and available solutions, represents a significant setback for African literary autonomy. As Hans Zell explained in 2015,

> Established with the generous financial support from several donor organisations and foundations, the principle aims of this scheme were to help overcome shortages of culturally relevant African-published books in African libraries, to promote an intra-African trade in books, raise awareness of African-published material, and support autonomous African publishers through sales via African Books Collective, who operated the scheme from 1991 to 2004, in later years in cooperation with Book Aid International (see Profile). The scheme consisted of two components: (1) The supply of adult fiction and children's books/teenage fiction to African public, school and community libraries. (2) Provision of scholarly/tertiary level African published titles to university libraries in Africa. Both components of the scheme were completely recipient-request led, through provision of catalogues and other selection tools made available to recipient libraries. By the scheme's end, an average of some 12,000 literary and children's titles and

7,000 scholarly titles had been donated each year (Zell 2015: 34).

A shift towards collaborative initiatives, where donors engage directly with African publishers and libraries to address needs articulated by Africans themselves, is a crucial step forward. This approach, which prioritises partnership over prescription, stands in stark contrast to the paternalistic model where donors dictate terms and claim to possess all the answers.

Entrenched stereotypes and a lack of support for African creativity stifle the publishing landscape. Even progressive publishers, including university presses, hesitate to champion diverse content, fearing financial losses if they deviate from predictable, standardised fare. This homogenising effect is further reinforced by the uncritical recruitment of reviewers, often without regard for ideological or cultural perspectives, effectively turning publishing into a tool for policing ideas and suppressing genuine diversity in the global book market (Nyamnjoh 2004, 2012, 2017).

The economics, culture, and politics of African publishing create a complex web of hierarchies that determine which publications are recognised and represented. Mediocrity, invisibility, poor publisher reputation, and inadequate marketing and distribution all contribute to the struggles of African writers and academics. These challenges, while universal, are particularly acute in Africa, exacerbated by the global popularity of negative representations of the continent and its creativity. African scholars in the humanities and social sciences often face a difficult choice between relevance and recognition, as the political economy of publishing often prevents them from achieving both (Nyamnjoh 2004; Mlambo 2007).

Publishers, driven primarily by economic considerations, are reluctant to promote diverse content at the risk of financial instability. Even seemingly "progressive" publishers prioritise economic survival over ideological diversity. The uncritical reliance on reviewers, regardless of their ideological leanings, underscores that publishing ultimately serves to police ideas and maintain a superficial plurality at the expense of genuine diversity.

The review process itself is a mechanism for enforcing established traditions and expectations. In a world marked by economic, cultural, and political hierarchies, the question arises: whose traditions and tastes are being enforced? The power to define and manage these standards often resides with those who hold economic capital, leading to the prioritisation of familiar cultural expressions over innovative or challenging ones. Publishers, editors, and reviewers, socialised within these hierarchies, often unconsciously minimise the scientific and creative capabilities of the African mind, even if this bias is not explicitly stated.

African artistic and scientific creativity faces a formidable challenge in gaining recognition. African publishing, often driven by economic, cultural, or political factors, perpetuates a global hierarchy that marginalises African voices. While many African publishers south of the Sahara lack the financial resources to promote diverse perspectives, even South African publishers, despite their stronger infrastructure, frequently prioritise Western viewpoints and reject contributions from elsewhere on the continent. This is starkly illustrated by my own experiences with two South African publishers and their reviewers of my manuscript, *The Travail of Dieudonné*.

Reviewers' comments on the author's manuscripts reveal a pattern. One reviewer acknowledged the work's accomplishment, stating, "This is by far the most accomplished of all this author's manuscripts that I have had the privilege of reading. Dieudonné has several very interesting strands which come together to form something which is original and entertaining."

However, they ultimately deemed it unpublishable due to perceived market limitations, arguing that "a book, even of this quality, may struggle in a South African market that continues to exhibit little interest in literature from elsewhere in Africa." Another reviewer, while recognising the manuscript's quality as "a further, and more fully realised, contribution to Francis Nyamnjoh's wide-angle critique of Cameroonian society," recommended rejection based on the author's "lack of profile" and the perception that "today's marketplace makes little space for novellas – even less for those originating from north of the Limpopo."[10]

The successful publication of the previously rejected manuscript by Chakava's East African Educational Publishers underscores the limitations of South African publishing's market-driven approach. This approach, which prioritises commercial viability, perpetuates negative stereotypes, stifles diversity, and risks cultural imperialism, hindering the development of an authentic African literary landscape.

African publishing's future demands a departure from this narrow focus. Traditions, like fiction, are dynamic and evolving. Just as reviewers encourage writers to revise, marginalised African voices urgently seek representation. African publishers must champion these voices, fostering a publishing ecosystem that reflects the continent's diverse identities and promotes cultural conviviality.

This vision necessitates a shift beyond purely market-driven considerations. Scholarly traditions are fluid, and publishers, both within and outside Africa, must actively populate the global market with diverse

---

[10] See Francis B. Nyamnjoh, "Pipers, Tunes and Global Hierarchies in African Publishing," *Bookmark: News Magazine of the South African Booksellers' Association*, July-September 2006, pp.29-30. See also, https://www.nyamnjoh.com/2006/08/pipers_tunes_an.html, accessed March 21, 2025.

African narratives. This demands creating space for powerful voices that challenge conventional wisdom.

Currently, inadequate investment in African knowledge and cultural production reinforces outdated stereotypes and hinders the creation of authentic African narratives. In a globalised world, combating this "cultural poverty" requires deliberate policies that support the production and consumption of African cultural products, empowering Africans to tell their own stories with dignity.

However, this mission clashes with a profit-driven global cultural industry that disregards cultural diversity. Publishers are crucial in eradicating this "cultural poverty" by actively disseminating African books as cultural artifacts. African publishers, particularly, bear the responsibility of representing the "rainbow continent," a task requiring sustained commitment and transformative action.

Chakava's legacy, including the enduring African Books Collective, has addressed external distribution challenges. Now, the focus must shift to internal distribution and leveraging e-publishing and print-on-demand technologies to unlock the potential of previously unviable titles (Jay 2007, 2016: 213-215; Aina & Mutula 2007; Wafawarowa 2007; Manji 2007). Chakava's passing should inspire a new era of concrete action, where support for African literature translates into a sustainable publishing ecosystem that empowers writers and provides culturally relevant educational resources for African children (Nyamnjoh 2004, 2008, 2012).

Chakava and the Language Question

Chakava's commitment to African languages transcended mere economic considerations. He firmly believed in their power to foster cultural identity and social growth. This belief manifested in several bold initiatives. Notably, he published Ngũgĩ wa Thiong'o's works in Gikuyu (Ngũgĩ wa Thiong'o 2016), despite the commercial risks involved and the fact that Heinemann, where he worked at the time, was under British ownership[11]. In the politically charged early 1980s, publishing Ngũgĩ wa Thiong'o's Gĩkũyũ plays was a perilous endeavour; "it was his plays, especially in Gĩkũyũ, which were to lead to his detention and ultimate exile" (Currey 2016: 38). Despite threats to his life, and subtle pressure from his London "bosses" to abandon the project, Henry Chakava remained resolute (Chakava 2018), leading Ngũgĩ wa Thiong'o to acknowledge their relationship as follows: "He[Chakava] was once my student whose papers I graded. Then he became my publisher who graded my manuscripts; but most important he became a friend who has stood by me in times of happiness and sorrow, even in those times when being seen with me was a dangerous thing" (Ngũgĩ wa Thiong'o 2016; 25).. His decision, made in the teeth of potential political backlash, epitomised his bravery, his dedication to providing a platform for African literature, and his bold challenge to the hegemony of colonial languages.[12]. Despite threats, censorship, and commercial struggles, publishing Ngũgĩ remained one of Chakava's greatest achievements, despite Ngũgĩ's reduced influence in Kenya because of his exile (Chakava 1996a; Ngũgĩ wa Thiong'o 2016).

Chakava played a pivotal role in establishing Kiswahili within the Kenyan education system by publishing essential course books. This strengthened Kiswahili's position as a bridge between English and other, often marginalised, African languages(Kamau

---

[11] Henry Chakava In Memoriam - Read African Books, accessed March 12, 2025, https://www.readafricanbooks.com/henry-chakava-in-memoriam/

[12] Henry Chakava | maisha yetu, accessed March 12, 2025, https://kenyanbooks.wordpress.com/tag/henry-chakava/

2016: 7-9)[13]. He envisioned Kiswahili as a unifying force, crucial for national development. Despite the low profitability of publishing in African languages, Chakava remained committed, recognising their inherent cultural and social value (Chakava 1977) [14]. Chakava's publications spanned oral literature (Currey 2008: xviii, 2016: 31-32), reflecting his commitment to integrating orality into African creative writing (Gikandi 2016: 53-55), language learning materials, and an English-Swahili dictionary [15]. It is fitting, then, that Mĩcere Gĩthae Mŭgo paid him the ultimate tribute in African orature, capturing his essence with these words:

> You, who have philosophised that Orature enables fast, easy and spontaneous communication of educational, cultural, and entertainment content across communities and generations as it traverses arenas of life and living. You, who have theorised that Orature represents the codified history and wisdom of communities. You, who have applauded Orature as a unique, inexpensive, but effective resource for development in communities that thrive on orate-ness. You, who have embalmed the art of the spoken word in print, giving it wings across the globe. (Mĩcere Gĩthae Mŭgo 2016: 59).

However, publishing in Indigenous African languages faces significant obstacles. Chakava, in 1977, highlighted challenges such as substantial local

[13] Dr Henry Chakava: Father of Kenyan publishing takes final bow - The Standard, accessed March 12, 2025, https://www.standardmedia.co.ke/national/article/2001491124/dr-henry-chakava-father-of-kenyan-publishing-takes-final-bow

[14] Henry Chakava In Memoriam - Read African Books, accessed March 12, 2025, https://www.readafricanbooks.com/henry-chakava-in-memoriam/

[15] Henry Chakava In Memoriam - Read African Books, accessed March 12, 2025, https://www.readafricanbooks.com/henry-chakava-in-memoriam/

variations within languages, the absence of standardised orthographies, and the resulting need for new symbols and fonts, which complicate readability. He also noted the limited pool of authors, readers, editors, and printers fluent in specific ethnic languages. This led him to promote Kiswahili as a practical lingua franca solution for Kenya (Chakava 1977). The challenges notwithstanding, by 2016, Chakava and the East African Educational Publishers had published not only in Gikuyu, but also "in five other local languages in Kenya: Dholuo, Kikamba, Ekegusii, Lugooli, and Kimeru", as well as "in seven Zambian local languages: Cibemba, Chitonga, Silozi, Chinyanja, Kiikaonde, Luvale and Lunda" (Kamau 2016: 9).

The legacy of colonial languages – English, French, Portuguese, and Spanish – continues to dominate education and scholarship, marginalising African languages. This entrenched system creates substantial resistance for African intellectuals advocating for the promotion of indigenous language publishing (Fonlon 2012 [1964]; Nyamnjoh 2016).

Organisations like CODESRIA, much like Chakava, grapple with these realities. As a pan-African entity, CODESRIA navigates diverse linguistic zones – Anglophone, Francophone, Lusophone, and Arabophone Africa – striving to enhance inclusivity through multilingual activities, translation, interpretation, and publications in Arabic, English, French, and Portuguese (Olukoshi & Nyamnjoh 2007; Nyamnjoh 2016).

Despite these efforts, persistent obstacles remain: resistance to mother tongue education, the dominance of colonial languages in higher education, and the influence of international curricula that prioritise European and North American languages. Colonial languages are imbued with a status that associates them with science, progress, and enlightenment, while African languages are relegated to mere rhetoric, their relevance to nation-building and development dismissed. In practice, they are often silenced, driven from the minds and mouths of African students and scholars. This legacy, as Ngũgĩ wa Thiong'o vividly illustrates in his writing on Kenya, has left an indelible mark. Postcolonial educators, inheriting condescending attitudes, continued to ban African languages in schools, elevate English as the medium of instruction, and even resort to corporal punishment and fines to suppress mother tongue usage (Ngũgĩ wa Thiong'o 1997: 620).

African intellectuals who dare to champion indigenous languages often find themselves swimming against a powerful current. Ali Mazrui's attempt to address the OAU in Kiswahili, one of Africa's most widely spoken languages, was met with bewildered incomprehension, as no translation facilities were available (Mazrui, 1986). This situation, sadly, has seen little improvement since Mazrui's time. Indeed, a telling indication of the enduring challenge is evident in Dr. Nkosazana Dlamini Zuma's 2014 address to the African Union. Her "e-mail from the future," written from 2063, revealed:

> Our eldest daughter, the linguist, still lectures in Kiswahili in Cabo Verde, at the headquarters of the Pan African Virtual University. Kiswahili is now a major African working language, and a global language taught at most faculties across the world. Our grandchildren find it very funny how we used to struggle at AU meetings with English, French and Portuguese interpretations, how we used to fight that the English version is not in line with the French or Arabic text! Now we have a lingua franca, and multi-lingualism is the order of the day.[16]

---

[16] http://cpauc.au.int/en/content/statement-he-dr-nkosazana-dlamini-zuma-chairperson-african-union-commission-twenty-second-ordinary-session accessed 12 February 2014.

Unlike nations such as Ethiopia, Tanzania, Kenya, Mali, Burkina Faso, Botswana, and South Africa, many African countries have yet to fully embrace the principle that literacy, even at the primary level, extends beyond fluency in European languages.

The adoption of policies promoting education in African languages remains limited. Even in countries with such policies, local languages are often relegated to adult literacy and primary/secondary education, effectively disconnecting universities from the broader population. With the notable exceptions of Tanzania and Ethiopia, and to some extent South Africa (considering Afrikaans), few African universities south of the Sahara offer comprehensive diploma programs with African languages as the primary medium of instruction (Crossman and Devisch 1999: 7; Chumbow 2005, 2009).

Debates surrounding mother tongue education in early schooling persist. While some countries have policies in place, implementation is often hindered by stakeholder resistance. Concerns about diluting educational standards and the need to prepare students for a globalised world, where colonial languages dominate higher education, fuel this resistance. This dynamic reflects the pervasive hegemony of these languages.

Language is fundamental to our experience. The absence of African languages in key domains is as significant as their presence. Cosmopolitanism and increased mobility raise complex questions about whose mother tongue takes precedence. Additionally, the elite's preference for private schools with international curricula further undermines the implementation of national language policies (Nyamnjoh 2012). Without personal investment in mother tongue education, policy implementation remains challenging.

While African speakers and writers have indeed domesticated colonial languages, achieving fluency that rivals native speakers, this success often comes at the expense of developing the languages that encapsulate the cultural experiences and worldviews of the wider population. This represents a profound and immeasurable loss to the economy of understanding (Nyamnjoh 2017; Nyamnjoh et al. 2021).

Chakava and Translation

Chakava's contribution to translation further solidified his commitment to promoting African literature. Recognising the linguistic diversity of the continent, he initiated the translation of major titles from the Heinemann African Writers Series into Kiswahili, and also facilitated some translation from Kiswahili into English[17]. This initiative broadened the accessibility of African literature, allowing readers across linguistic boundaries to engage with works by renowned authors such as Chinua Achebe, Ngũgĩ wa Thiong'o, and Elechi Amadi[18], even when these translations were not commercially viable (Chakava 1977). By facilitating cross-cultural exchange through translation, Chakava enriched the literary landscape and fostered a deeper appreciation for African narratives.

However, both Chakava's efforts highlight the challenges associated with translation. These include the difficulty in finding accomplished and competent translators, the need to balance accuracy with reflecting the spirit of a document, and the logistical complexities of coordinating translation projects.

---

[17] Remembering Chakava: The man who gave a voice to a new generation of African writers, accessed March 12, 2025, https://eastleighvoice.co.ke/national/25870/remembering-chakava:-the-man-who-gave-a-voice-to-a-new-generation-of-african-writers

[18] Ngũgĩ wa Thiong'o: Henry Chakava - My friend, student and saviour - Daily Nation, accessed March 12, 2025, https://nation.africa/kenya/news/ng%C5%A9g%C4%A9-wa-thiong-o-henry-chakava-my-friend-student-and-saviour-4552952

Translation Dilemmas

While investing in translation is essential, quality remains a persistent challenge due to the scarcity of skilled translators. During my time at CODESRIA, Executive Committee members frequently lamented the poor quality and inaccuracies of French and Portuguese translations of English documents – the Executive Secretary's working language[19]. Time was consistently spent correcting minutes and addressing these concerns. It was often emphasised that translations should prioritise capturing the spirit of a document over strict academic correctness. The Executive Secretary acknowledged these issues, noting the inherent complexities of translation, even for experts. However, tight deadlines often compromised quality, and in-house translations, though coordinated by an accredited translator, faced similar constraints[20].

Within CODESRIA's Publications Programme, planning is inherently unpredictable. Unlike organising conferences or research networks, book publishing is fraught with uncertainties. A reliable translator might be unavailable at critical moments, forcing CODESRIA to seek less ideal alternatives. While

---

[19] On reading an earlier draft of this paper, Edith Félicité Koumtoudji, a doctoral student in Translation at the University of Witwatersrand, made the following pertinent remark, "Quality translation requires sufficient time to translate, among other things. Are the translators given enough time or documents are sent to them at the last minute? It is also always important to indicate the brief for any translation project: who is the target audience and what purpose the translated document is going to serve."

[20] Given the volume of translation CODESRIA regularly does, the need for such an in-house translation unit with someone to coordinate the work carried out by the various translators is clearly preferred rather than merely having to depend on freelance translators on an ad hoc basis. Over the years, the CODESRIA translation unit has compiled its own terminology database to assist translators working for the organisation

maintaining a pool of translators is desirable, long-term contracts are financially prohibitive for a donor-dependent organisation like CODESRIA. Even when available, translators' workloads may hinder adherence to deadlines. Replacing them with potentially less competent individuals is rarely a viable solution. The scarcity of social science specialists among translators further complicates matters. CODESRIA, while often urgent, may not always be the most competitive client.

The *Africa Review of Books* project faced significant hurdles in coordinating its multilingual collaboration, evidenced by the challenges of managing four institutions spanning four countries: CODESRIA in Dakar, FSS in Addis Ababa, CRASC in Tunis, and UNISA Press in Pretoria. Communication breakdowns became apparent during the production of the inaugural issue, handled by FSS and printed by UNISA. The resulting publication contained numerous errors, most notably the complete omission of the French title ('*Revue Africaine des Livres*'), which created a misleading impression of an exclusively English-language journal. The project's initial 2003 meeting in Addis Ababa, as documented in the minutes, had presciently anticipated such issues, stipulating the production of separate English and French editions after the first two issues.

This item was discussed in detail and it was agreed that, for the first two issues, a single *Review* will be published in English and French in a joint format to reflect the continent's linguistic diversity. In the long term, efforts will be made to explore the possibility of producing separate English and French versions of the *Review*, with FSS being responsible for the former and CRASC for the latter. In this particular case, Editorial messages and landmark articles will be translated interchangeably and featured in both versions to ensure a balanced coverage.

The inherent challenges of translation are well-documented, familiar to both students and professionals (Venuti 2004; Ndi 2008). These experts recognise the limitations of literal, decontextualised translations, advocating instead for capturing the spirit of the original text. The crucial role of contextual understanding becomes evident, as meaning is complex and concepts are not always directly transferable between languages.

Thorsten Pattberg, in his article "Language Imperialism, Concepts and Civilisation: China versus The West," highlights this issue. He asserts that "over 35,000 Chinese words or phrases...cannot properly be translated into the English language" and argues that European languages, rooted in distinct histories and traditions, are inadequate for conveying Chinese concepts. Consequently, he suggests adopting, rather than translating, key foreign terms. This stance aligns with the notion that "the idiosyncratic use of language makes it difficult for linguistic concepts to be universalised" (Ndi 2008:113).

Despite these concerns, translation persists, often driven by a desire for credentialism or legitimation. As Pattberg argues in "China: Lost in Translation," applying terms like "philosophy" in contexts where they don't fully apply inadvertently reinforces Western dominance in interpreting non-Western thought. Such attempts by local scholars to mimic Western frameworks, whether intentional or not, contribute to the "Western onslaught on...terminology" and perpetuate Western control over intellectual discourse. Faced with the choice between flawed translation for superficial understanding and no translation at all, the former often prevails. This empowers local scholars seeking Western validation, while marginalising those who champion indigenous terminologies. These latter scholars, deemed non-compliant with Western standards, are often excluded from mainstream global discourse.[21]

Similar concerns arise regarding the vast array of indigenous African languages, many of which, unlike Chinese, are still developing written forms. Munyaradzi Mawere, cited in Nyamnjoh (2016) as Associate Professor at Universidade Pedagogica in Mozambique at the time, while acknowledging CODESRIA's significant role in promoting African scholarship since 1973, expresses frustration over its failure to integrate major indigenous African languages into its activities, knowledge production, and dissemination. He poses a critical question:

> Given the translation challenges highlighted by Thorsten Pattberg with regard to Chinese, what is CODESRIA's vision for African indigenous languages? Must Africa perpetually rely on colonial languages for research and dissemination? While CODESRIA fosters research by African scholars, it has neglected indigenous languages. After 40 years, it should have published, or at least begun publishing, in languages like Swahili, Shona, or Hausa, demonstrating a genuine commitment to their promotion. Currently, its exclusive use of colonial languages – English, French, and Portuguese –suggests otherwise. If, in the name of globalisation, Africans are compelled to use colonial languages, why can't Europeans and Americans reciprocate by engaging with African languages to understand the continent? CODESRIA should expand beyond its four working languages to include languages like Swahili, Zulu, Gikuyu, and Hausa.

Mawere's concerns echo the persistent critique of English language dominance in Kenya, where the educational system, inheriting colonial biases, continues to suppress African languages. As Ngũgĩ wa

---

[21] See Thorsten Pattberg, "China: Lost in Translation" http://www.atimes.com/atimes/China/NG24Dj02.html, accessed 20 February 2014.

Thiong'o illustrates, schools "ban African languages...and elevate English as the medium of instruction," resorting to punishment for mother tongue usage (Ngũgĩ wa Thiong'o 1997: 620). Ngũgĩ himself champions Gikuyu, writing and publishing his novels in his mother tongue before translating them into English. He metaphorically describes colonial languages as a "third leg," an artificial appendage (Ngũgĩ wa Thiong'o 2005).

It is important to acknowledge that many Africans, beyond the elite, are multilingual, adept at navigating multiple worldviews. However, this linguistic versatility should not excuse the continued marginalisation of indigenous languages.

Despite the acknowledged challenges and imperfections of translation – the age-old adage 'to translate is to betray' – linguistic exchange remains indispensable. While sign language and other symbolic forms are valuable, they cannot fully satisfy our communicative needs. We choose to embrace the inevitable imperfections of translation rather than forgo its benefits entirely.

Hamid Dabashi's "Found in Translation"[22] offers a comforting perspective. Dabashi argues that philosophical and literary works, far from being diminished, "gain far more than they lose in translation." He posits that translation allows authors to breathe in new linguistic spaces and exposes their work to a broader, unfamiliar audience.

Dabashi further contends that even flawed translations can bring works and thinkers into prominence, rescuing them from obscurity. He cites Heidegger as an example, whose French translators and

---

[22] Hamid Dabashi is the Hagop Kevorkian Professor of Iranian Studies and Comparative Literature at Columbia University in New York. See http://opinionator.blogs.nytimes.com/author/hamid-dabashi/ accessed 18 February 2014

commentators were crucial in disseminating his work. Similarly, Derrida's interpretation of Heidegger, reaching an English-speaking audience, played a pivotal role in shaping contemporary Continental philosophy. Dabashi attributes this not to the inherent superiority of any language, but to the "imperial power and reach" of dominant languages.

This collaborative aspect of translation is inherently valuable. Applying this to African scholarship, and CODESRIA's efforts, we must ask: what would our understanding of Africa be without access to even imperfect representations of our own narratives, albeit in colonial languages? With little success in the development of indigenous and endogenous languages despite early and repeated clarion postcolonial calls to this end, much scientific production, activity and collaboration among scholars across the continent continues to be mediated by these so-called colonial languages. Translations of works by leading African scholars like Paulin Hountondji, Mahmood Mamdani, and Achille Mbembe, as well as classics like *The Meanings of Timbuktu* (Jeppie and Bachir 2008), have expanded access to African knowledge (Nyamnjoh 2016).

CODESRIA, by promoting research and publications in its four working languages, fosters intellectual exchange among Africans, overcoming linguistic barriers. Translation enables a truly pan-African scholarship, granting access to knowledge regardless of linguistic origin. While unintended misinterpretations may occur, the value of translated texts should not be underestimated (Nyamnjoh 2016).

The philosophical debate surrounding language underscores that translation is a process of negotiation and reinterpretation. Given the diverse perspectives that shape understanding, perfect translation is an unattainable ideal. Yet, from this perspective, translation ultimately does more good than harm. African scholars, through initiatives like CODESRIA, navigate the constraints of colonial languages and geographies while simultaneously transcending them (Nyamnjoh 2016).

Founding Member of the African Books Collective

Beyond his dedication to Kenyan publishing, Chakava recognised the vital role of collaboration and wider distribution for African books. He was a founding member of the African Books Collective (ABC), established in 1989 following an initial brainstorming 1985 London meeting funded by the Swedish International Development Agency (SIDA) [23]. ABC, an Oxford-based UK non-profit marketing and distribution outlet, is a "publishers' own collective UK company," owned and governed by "the original founders" (Jay 2016: 205-207), and dedicated to promoting African publishers' books globally. Collaborating with publishers from across Africa, including CODESRIA in Dakar, Victor Nwankwo of Fourth Dimension Publishing in Nigeria, and Walter Bgoya of Mkuki na Nyota Publishers in Tanzania, Chakava helped shape ABC into a platform that amplified African voices and facilitated the international dissemination of African literature and scholarship (Jay 2016: 205-216) [24].

I first met him in 2004 at the ABC board meeting in Oxford. I had just been appointed Senior Programme Officer in charge of publications at CODESRIA.

---

[23] Henry Chakava: an annotated bibliography | Africa Bibliography ..., accessed March 12, 2025, https://www.cambridge.org/core/journals/africa-bibliography-research-and-documentation/article/henry-chakava-an-annotated-bibliography/9282345B7FB1BB6F8D51376CB5F31D73

[24] Henry Chakava In Memoriam - Read African Books, accessed March 12, 2025, https://www.readafricanbooks.com/henry-chakava-in-memoriam/

Chakava was on the ABC board in his capacity as a founding member and chairperson of East African Educational Publishers (EAEP), while I was representing CODESRIA.

It did not take more than an initial conversation for me to see that Chakava's vision and commitment to promoting African writers and publishing African scholarship dovetailed perfectly with CODESRIA's own vision (Nyamnjoh 2016).

During my six years on the board of ABC, it was an infinite pleasure and privilege to work with Chakava, a man of great wisdom and experience, who inspired and spurred me on in my own dedication to help fulfil CODESRIA's ambition and mission as a leading scholarly publisher in Africa, and eventually as well, my enthusiasm and dedication to Langaa Research and Publishing Common Initiative Group, an institute I co-founded in 2004. Through him, two of my novels – *A Nose for Money* (2006) and *The Travail of Dieudonné* (2008) – were published by East African Educational Publishers.

Other Contributions to African Publishing

Beyond his work with EAEP and unrelenting advocacy for greater cooperation among publishers, government support for local publishing, and policy reforms to strengthen the industry in Kenya[25], Chakava made significant contributions to the development of the African publishing landscape. He was instrumental in founding the African Publishing Institute (API) and the Jomo Kenyatta Prize for Literature[26]. The API, with its partnerships with organisations like the Dag Hammarskjöld Foundation, the World Bank, and

---

[25] Henry Chakava, "Publishing in Kenya", *Africa Bibliography*. 1989;1988:vi-xiv. doi:10.1017/S0266673100005006

[26] Henry Chakava - Wikipedia, accessed March 12, 2025, https://en.wikipedia.org/wiki/Henry_Chakava

others, aimed to enhance African literature through training and development programmes. The Jomo Kenyatta Prize for Literature, established in collaboration with the Text Book Centre, recognised and celebrated outstanding literary works by Kenyan authors (Kamau 2016: 10-11).

Henry Chakava, a "firm believer in unity of purpose" (Kamau 2016: 10), was a driving force behind key networks that transformed African literature and publishing. He played a crucial role in establishing the Pan African Writers' Association (PAWA), the African Publishers Network (APNET), the African Booksellers Association (PABA), and the African Books Collective (ABC). These late 1980s and early 1990s initiatives aimed to address the systemic challenges hindering African writers, particularly those working in indigenous languages, by improving publishing capacity and distribution (Nyariki 2016). Chakava's dedication to nurturing talent and fostering a vibrant literary culture is evident in these efforts.

His contribution to APNET deserves particular attention, especially considering his passion for book festivals. He was instrumental in founding the Zimbabwe International Book Fair (including its Indaba discussion sessions) and the Nairobi International Book Fair, and he actively supported colleagues in establishing similar events across the continent. These book fairs served as vital platforms for promoting African literature and fostering industry connections.

In 1992, mirroring the establishment of the East African Educational Publishers (EAEP), the African Publishers Network (APNET) was formed, providing a unified platform for indigenous African publishers. This pan-African organisation aimed to bolster collective capacity through networking, training, and trade promotion – essential components for a flourishing African publishing sector.

Henry Chakava played a pivotal role in APNET's formation, leveraging his extensive experience to address the sector's pressing challenges. The network's emphasis on information sharing and collaboration naturally fostered capacity building and professional development, solidifying training as a core mission.

Prior to APNET, African publishers faced significant isolation, hindering collaboration and knowledge exchange. Multinational dominance marginalised local voices, while complex production, distribution, and marketing hurdles further impeded growth. Limited training opportunities, compounded by economic constraints and restrictive government policies, exacerbated these issues.

These multifaceted challenges prompted a collective response. African publishers convened conferences and seminars, culminating in APNET's founding in Harare, Zimbabwe, in 1992. This landmark event, bringing together delegates from nine countries, marked a crucial step towards cooperation and professionalisation. The pre-existing challenges, particularly the lack of training infrastructure and the influence of external entities, underscored the necessity of APNET's focused training mandate.

Henry Chakava, consistently recognised as a founder, was central to APNET's genesis. As a respected publisher, his presence lent credibility and direction to the nascent organization. His experience, dating back to 1972, informed APNET's objectives and strategies, and his extensive networks mobilised crucial support, fostering collective ownership.

Chakava's vision for a thriving African publishing industry, encompassing linguistic diversity, indigenous ownership, and professional excellence, directly aligned with APNET's training focus. He recognised the urgent need for skilled professionals across all publishing disciplines. His founding of the African Publishing Institute (API), dedicated to enhancing African literature through training, further exemplifies his commitment to capacity building. His articulation of an "Autonomous African Publishing House" underscored the critical importance of a skilled workforce [27].

APNET's commitment to training, shaped by figures like Chakava, included investigating training needs and organising training for publishers. The network adopted the API curriculum, conducting over 30 workshops in 18 countries, demonstrating a substantial commitment to practical training. Programmes like "APNET Training for Trainers in Tanzania" exemplified a strategic approach to sustainable capacity building, reflecting Chakava's vision of self-reliance. APNET's long-term objectives, including strengthening training resources and partnering with universities, underscored this commitment.

Chakava's expertise continued to shape APNET's direction. His reputation enhanced its credibility, attracting members and securing funding. His emphasis on training ensured its centrality in APNET's strategy. The establishment of a research and documentation centre further supported ongoing development. His involvement in organisations like the African Books Collective (ABC) fostered a sustainable and impactful APNET. Its evolution into a diverse network, with ongoing activities, demonstrates the robustness of its foundational principles.

Chakava's writings, including his paper "An Autonomous African Publishing House: A Model," explicitly addressed the necessity of training.[28] His

---

[27] Walter Bgoya, "Henry Chakava (1946 – 2024): The publisher who pricked the people into consciousness", https://africanarguments.org/2024/04/henry-chakava-the-publisher-who-pricked-the-people-into-consciousness/, accessed March 19, 2025.

[28] Walter Bgoya, "Henry Chakava (1946 – 2024): The publisher who pricked the people into consciousness", https://africanarguments.org/2024/04/henry-chakava-the-

quotes emphasised continuous learning and quality materials, highlighting the need for skilled professionals. His focus on indigenous language publishing further underscored this need.

The significant impact of APNET and the pivotal contributions of Henry Chakava are well-documented in scholarly literature. Critical context is provided by annotated bibliographies of Chakava's work, as well as analyses of the challenges facing African publishing. Notably, the festschrift *Coming of Age: Strides in African Publishing* (Kamau & Mitambo, 2016), featuring contributions from fellow publishers, writers, and academics, stands as a testament to his profound influence. These works collectively underscore APNET's crucial role and Chakava's prominent position in fostering the growth of indigenous publishing.

Chakava's instrumental role in the creation and subsequent success of APNET is undeniable. His experience and visionary leadership shaped APNET's focus on training, most notably through the integration of the African Publishing Institute (API) curriculum into its workshops. This direct influence, coupled with his commitment to professional development as evidenced by the API and his extensive writings, firmly established training as a cornerstone of APNET's strategic approach. Chakava's enduring legacy is clearly reflected in APNET's continued impact on the African publishing industry.

Chakava's Writings on Publishing

Chakava was more than a publisher; he was a pioneering intellectual in African literature and philosophy, for whom "publishing was not just a business defined by markets and regulation, but also an

---

publisher-who-pricked-the-people-into-consciousness/, accessed March 19, 2025.

intellectual and creative enterprise" (Gikandi 2016: 47). He ensured that one of the priorities of the East African Educational Publishers was scholarly publishing, which included monographs, journals and edited collections (Chakava 2007; Ilieva and Chakava 2016). His influential 1996 book, *Publishing in Africa: One Man's Perspective* (Chakava 1996b)[29], with an introduction by Chinua Achebe, offers an authoritative analysis of the African publishing landscape. It explores critical aspects of the industry, including the role of indigenous languages, the necessity of government support, and the development of local publishing capacity, demonstrating his profound understanding and dedication to its advancement.

Furthermore, Chakava's influence and contributions were recognised by his peers through the publication of a festschrift in his honour, *Coming of Age: Strides in African Publishing* (Kamau & Mitambo 2016)[30]. This collection of essays, written by prominent figures in African literature and publishing, pays tribute to his significant role in shaping the industry.

Finally, Chakava played a crucial role in drafting the Kenyan copyright act[31]. This contribution helped shape the legal framework for publishing in Kenya, ensuring the protection of intellectual property rights for authors and publishers.

Henry Chakava's unwavering dedication to promoting African publishing and championing the rights of African writers stood as a defiant counterpoint to the global dominance of Western models. Through East African Educational Publishers, he tirelessly

---

[29] See also, Henry Chakava - Wikipedia, accessed March 12, 2025, https://en.wikipedia.org/wiki/Henry_Chakava

[30] See also, Henry Chakava In Memoriam - Read African Books, accessed March 12, 2025, https://www.readafricanbooks.com/henry-chakava-in-memoriam/

[31] Henry Chakava - Wikipedia, accessed March 12, 2025, https://en.wikipedia.org/wiki/Henry_Chakava

advocated for the integration of African perspectives and voices into African education. He passionately argued that African publishers have a crucial responsibility to provide books that inform and enlighten young Africans, who are often caught between the imperative of reviving fading traditions and the allure of a pervasive Western consumer culture. His career, from his early days with Heinemann, resembles a relentless ascent of a Kilimanjaro of economic, cultural, and political obstacles, all in the pursuit of authentic and relevant African publishing.

Regrettably, Chakava's message has often been met with indifference. Many African publishers, struggling for survival, prioritise the safer path of standardised textbooks, guaranteeing modest profits without challenging the status quo (Ojeniyi 2016). In a precarious industry, even multinational corporations face economic vulnerability. Consequently, works of fiction that address African realities and offer alternative perspectives are frequently overlooked. As Chakava lamented, editors often lack the time and patience to guide authors in revising their work to an acceptable standard[32].

In a 2008 reflection, Henry Chakava observed that despite some progress, African publishing, since the pivotal 1973 Ile-Ife conference, presents a mixed picture. The 1970s' growth gave way to a decline in the 1980s, followed by a gradual resurgence in the 1990s. While writer, publisher, and bookseller associations have proliferated, and book fairs have increased, these entities often remain structurally weak, dependent on

---

[32] According to Henry Chakava, Chairman of East African Educational Publishers, Nairobi, Kenya, Chakava, Henry "African Publishing: From Ile-Ife to the Present. " In P*ublishing, Books & Reading in Sub-Saharan Africa: A Critical Bibliography*, edited by Hans M. Zell. Lochcarron, Scotland: Hans Zell Publishing, 2018, xxxvii-l. https://www.hanszell.co.uk/Site/PDFs/Chakava,%20Introductory%20essay%20in%20PBRSSA,%202018.pdf (freely accessible).

donor support. Despite post-1990s initiatives, Africa's book production lags significantly behind global standards. The challenges of the 1970s and 1980s – capital shortages, lack of training, equipment, and raw materials, underdeveloped markets, and multinational competition – persist, albeit in diminished form. [33]

Chakava remained optimistic, despite the myriad obstacles facing African publishing: mediocre content, technical deficiencies, language barriers, publisher invisibility, and inadequate marketing and distribution. These universal issues are amplified in Africa by censorship, repression, limited training, unfavourable environments, and political obstacles. Governments, Chakava noted, prioritise book availability over the development of local publishing industries. Repressive climates have stifled local publishing and quality, forcing publishers to avoid controversial material, leading to business failures or the production of unprofitable, inoffensive literature.

These factors contribute to Africa's underdeveloped publishing sector, which accounts for a mere three percent of global book output and heavily relies on school textbooks and donor-funded programmes. Estimates indicate that approximately 95% of books published across the continent are for the education sector[34]. This contrasts sharply with regions like Europe, where the ratio of textbooks to non-textbooks

---

[33] According to Henry Chakava, Chairman of East African Educational Publishers, Nairobi, Kenya, Chakava, Henry "African Publishing: From Ile-Ife to the Present. " In P*ublishing, Books & Reading in Sub-Saharan Africa: A Critical Bibliography*, edited by Hans M. Zell. Lochcarron, Scotland: Hans Zell Publishing, 2018, xxxvii-l. https://www.hanszell.co.uk/Site/PDFs/Chakava,%20Introductory%20essay%20in%20PBRSSA,%202018.pdf (freely accessible).

[34] A good reading culture: Potential game changer in Africa - Read African Books, accessed March 20, 2025, https://www.readafricanbooks.com/opinion/a-good-reading-culture-potential-game-changer-in-africa/

is around 60:40[35]. This overwhelming focus on educational publishing suggests a significant prioritisation of meeting educational needs, which has a notable impact on the diversity of literary content accessible to African readers and the broader development of a reading culture that extends beyond academic requirements[36]. While the need for textbooks to improve literacy is undeniable, the sheer volume compared to other genres points to a publishing landscape heavily oriented towards education. Efforts to improve the student-to-textbook ratio in countries like Cameroon[37] further underscore the critical role and volume of textbook publishing in addressing fundamental educational needs. Historical data, although limited, also suggests a long-standing trend of lower overall book production in Africa compared to other regions[38], implying that the majority of this limited output has historically been concentrated in essential educational materials. Challenges related to textbook budgets, quality, and distribution, as highlighted by UNESCO and the World Bank[39], further emphasise the central and often complex role

---

[35] A good reading culture: Potential game changer in Africa - Read African Books, accessed March 20, 2025, https://www.readafricanbooks.com/opinion/a-good-reading-culture-potential-game-changer-in-africa/

[36] A good reading culture: Potential game changer in Africa - Read African Books, accessed March 20, 2025, https://www.readafricanbooks.com/opinion/a-good-reading-culture-potential-game-changer-in-africa/

[37] Turning Pages, Transforming Lives: Cameroon's Textbook Revolution - World Bank, accessed March 20, 2025, https://www.worldbank.org/en/results/2024/02/01/turning-pages-transforming-lives-cameroon-textbook-revolution

[38] Book development in Africa; problems and perspectives - UNESCO Digital Library, accessed March 20, 2025, https://unesdoc.unesco.org/ark:/48223/pf0000059548

[39] UNESCO Documents Africa's Need for Textbooks - VOA, accessed March 20, 2025, https://www.voanews.com/a/unesco-documents-africa-need-textbooks/3179953.html

of textbook publishing in the African educational ecosystem. The significant proportion of textbook publishing likely means that financial and human resources within the industry are primarily directed towards this sector, potentially leaving less capacity for the development and promotion of other forms of literature. This focus could inadvertently limit the opportunities for authors exploring different genres and the representation of a wider spectrum of African stories and creativity.

Regarding the control of the publishing market in South Africa, research indicates a significant level of multinational dominance, particularly within the educational sector. It is reported that multinationals control 60% of educational publishing in South Africa, which constitutes a substantial 80% of the entire publishing industry in the country[40]. The remaining 40% of the total publishing market is largely dominated by local white-owned companies (30%), with black-owned companies accounting for a much smaller share (10%)[41]. This market structure highlights the considerable influence of international corporations in the South African publishing landscape, especially in the economically significant educational segment. Given that South Africa is identified as the leading publisher of books in Africa and possesses the continent's largest book market[42], the control exerted within this market has far-reaching implications for the broader African publishing industry. The total revenue

---

[40] UNESCO Documents Africa's Need for Textbooks - VOA, accessed March 20, 2025, https://www.voanews.com/a/unesco-documents-africa-need-textbooks/3179953.html

[41] UNESCO Documents Africa's Need for Textbooks - VOA, accessed March 20, 2025, https://www.voanews.com/a/unesco-documents-africa-need-textbooks/3179953.html

[42] Literature Industry Statistics in Africa - SME Blue Pages, accessed March 20, 2025, https://smebluepages.com/literature-industry-statistics-in-africa/

of the South African publishing market was estimated at $681.4 million in 2021, with books comprising the largest segment at $506.0 million[43]. This substantial financial value underscores the economic significance of the market share held by different entities. Major international publishers such as Pearson South Africa, Oxford University Press Southern Africa, Cambridge University Press South Africa, Macmillan South Africa, and Penguin Random House South Africa have a strong presence in the South African market[44], further confirming the involvement of multinational players. The acquisition of Random House Struik by Penguin Random House[45] illustrates a trend of consolidation and increasing multinational control within the South African publishing sector. The significant control held by multinational corporations in the educational publishing sector in South Africa likely restricts the market share available to local, particularly black-owned, publishers. The dominance of established international players creates considerable barriers for smaller domestic businesses seeking to compete effectively. Furthermore, because educational publishing represents such a large portion of the total publishing activity in South Africa, the control over this segment effectively grants multinationals significant influence over the entire book market, shaping its

---

[43] South Africa Publishing Market Summary, Competitive Analysis and Forecast, 2017-2026, accessed March 20, 2025, https://www.researchandmarkets.com/reports/5741249/south-africa-publishing-market-summary

[44] South Africa's Industry for the Publishing of Books and Other Publications, 2019, accessed March 20, 2025, https://www.globenewswire.com/news-release/2020/02/06/1981005/0/en/South-Africa-s-Industry-for-the-Publishing-of-Books-and-Other-Publications-2019.html

[45] Penguin Random House Acquires Full Ownership of South Africa's Random House Struik, accessed March 20, 2025, https://global.penguinrandomhouse.com/press-release/penguin-random-house-acquires-full-ownership-of-south-africas-random-house-struik/

direction and the types of content that are prioritised. The sustained presence of major international publishers in South Africa, likely attracted by the market's size and economic stability, indicates a continuing trend of multinational dominance in the foreseeable future.

Publishing for the majority of Africans is rare, with multinationals primarily serving an elite. Multinational publishers in Africa are often observed to target an elite demographic capable of reading and writing in European languages[46]. Consequently, the publication of books relevant to the interests and experiences of the majority of Africans is reported to be uncommon[47]. Historically, foreign-owned companies have dominated educational publishing, with publishing decisions frequently made outside the continent, potentially failing to reflect local needs and cultural contexts[48]. The heavy emphasis on textbook publishing, predominantly in official languages, coupled with the small market share for leisure reading, suggests a limited scope of publishing that caters to the broader population beyond educational requirements[49]. Factors such as low reading culture, the scarcity of libraries, and the limited presence of books in households, particularly non-

---

[46] UNESCO Documents Africa's Need for Textbooks - VOA, accessed March 20, 2025, https://www.voanews.com/a/unesco-documents-africa-need-textbooks/3179953.html

[47] The State Of African Publishing - ARB - مركز البحث في الأنثروبولوجيا الاجتماعية والثقافية, accessed March 20, 2025, https://arb.crasc.dz/index.php/ar/%D8%A7%D9%84%D8%A3%D8%B1%D9%82%D8%A7%D9%85/135-the-state-of-african-publishing

[48] Publishing in Africa from Independence to the Present Day - Read African Books, accessed March 20, 2025, https://www.readafricanbooks.com/opinion/publishing-in-africa-from-independence-to-the-present-day/

[49] A good reading culture: Potential game changer in Africa - Read African Books, accessed March 20, 2025, https://www.readafricanbooks.com/opinion/a-good-reading-culture-potential-game-changer-in-africa/

textbooks[50], further highlight the challenges in making books accessible to the general population. For instance, over 40% of households in South Africa report having no books at home[51]. While there is a growing demand for children's books in African indigenous languages and initiatives supporting local language storytelling[52], this indicates an effort to address an existing gap rather than a current widespread reality. The tendency of multinational publishers to focus on audiences proficient in European languages creates a linguistic and cultural barrier that limits access to books for a significant portion of the African population. This historical focus on certain markets and languages has led to the development of infrastructure and distribution networks that may not effectively reach broader populations, thus perpetuating the limited accessibility of publishing for the majority. Even if more books were published catering to the majority, the prevailing low book ownership and reading habits suggest that addressing these underlying issues would be crucial to truly improve accessibility.

The notion that multinational content reinforces a global hierarchy where African creativity is undervalued has historical roots and continues to be a subject of discussion. Some research suggests that multinational publishers in Africa have historically reproduced content informed by a global hierarchy that positions

---

[50] "Africa has no shortage of celebrated writers — so why is it so hard for African readers to get hold of their books? | by Pa Ikhide | Jan, 2025 | Medium, accessed March 20, 2025, https://medium.com/@ikhide/reading-culture-and-the-fate-of-the-book-in-africa-6abb6ce40b53

[51] More than 40 per cent of households surveyed have no books at home - UNICEF, accessed March 20, 2025, https://www.unicef.org/southafrica/press-releases/more-40-cent-households-surveyed-have-no-books-home

[52] Study on the Publishing Landscapes in Sub-Saharan Africa, accessed March 20, 2025, https://internationalpublishers.org/study-on-the-publishing-landscapes-in-sub-saharan-africa/

African creativity as less valuable, potentially due to economic, cultural, or political considerations[53]. Their focus on publishing in European languages for an elite audience can further perpetuate this dynamic. The historical practice of publishing decisions being made in the "north" and the initial scarcity of African-originated content[54] lend credence to the idea that a global hierarchy might have been historically reinforced through publishing (Nyamnjoh 2004, 2008, 2012, 2017). However, the emergence of independent African publishers and a growing global interest in diverse narratives [55] indicate a shift in this landscape. Local efforts are actively working to promote and value African stories and voices. The increasing global success of African creatives in fields like music and film[56] may also positively influence the publishing industry by generating greater demand for African literature and challenging existing biases within the global publishing market. Nonetheless, the fact that many successful African artists are often signed to European or North American labels[57] raises questions

---

[53] Africa And Publishing: Reflections - Pambazuka News, accessed March 20, 2025, https://pambazuka.org/governance/africa-and-publishing-reflections

[54] Publishing in Africa from Independence to the Present Day - Read African Books, accessed March 20, 2025, https://www.readafricanbooks.com/opinion/publishing-in-africa-from-independence-to-the-present-day/

[55] Study on the Publishing Landscapes in Sub-Saharan Africa, accessed March 20, 2025, https://internationalpublishers.org/study-on-the-publishing-landscapes-in-sub-saharan-africa/

[56] How Africa's creative economy is driving transformation - African Business, accessed March 20, 2025, https://african.business/2024/10/long-reads/how-africas-creative-economy-is-driving-transformation

[57] How Africa's creative economy is driving transformation - African Business, accessed March 20, 2025, https://african.business/2024/10/long-reads/how-africas-creative-economy-is-driving-transformation

about the capacity of African publishers to fully capitalise on this growing global interest and ensure that the benefits are primarily realised within the continent. While historical practices might have contributed to the undervaluation of African creativity, the current situation is characterised by a dynamic tension between the influence of multinationals and the growing strength and recognition of indigenous African creative expression.

African publishers south of the Sahara in particular face a multitude of challenges, particularly a lack of resources that hinders their ability to promote diverse works and ensure their long-term viability. These challenges include limited access to financing and undercapitalisation[58], weak distribution systems that struggle to reach readers effectively[59], high production costs for printing and raw materials[60], and intense competition from well-established multinational corporations[61]. The low purchasing power of the general population[62] and low literacy rates in European

---

[58] Publishing in Africa from Independence to the Present Day - Read African Books, accessed March 20, 2025, https://www.readafricanbooks.com/opinion/publishing-in-africa-from-independence-to-the-present-day/

[59] Publishing in Africa from Independence to the Present Day - Read African Books, accessed March 20, 2025, https://www.readafricanbooks.com/opinion/publishing-in-africa-from-independence-to-the-present-day/

[60] Literature Industry Statistics in Africa - SME Blue Pages, accessed March 20, 2025, https://smebluepages.com/literature-industry-statistics-in-africa/

[61] AFRICA AND PUBLISHING: REFLECTIONS - Pambazuka News, accessed March 20, 2025, https://pambazuka.org/governance/africa-and-publishing-reflections

[62] Publishing in Africa from Independence to the Present Day - Read African Books, accessed March 20, 2025, https://www.readafricanbooks.com/opinion/publishing-in-africa-from-independence-to-the-present-day/

languages[63] further complicate the market. Inadequate government support and policies, including the absence of strong national book policies and weak enforcement of copyright laws, also pose significant obstacles[64]. The prevalence of book piracy leads to substantial revenue losses for publishers[65]. Additionally, foreign exchange constraints can hinder international sales and procurement[66], and there is often a lack of sufficient training and infrastructure within the local publishing and printing industries[67]. The reliance on donor funding by some publishers[68] highlights the financial vulnerabilities within the sector. In response to these economic hurdles, African publishers are increasingly turning to alternative funding mechanisms such as crowdfunding and grants[69]. The numerous challenges faced especially by

---

63 Publishing in Africa from Independence to the Present Day - Read African Books, accessed March 20, 2025, https://www.readafricanbooks.com/opinion/publishing-in-africa-from-independence-to-the-present-day/

64 Publishing in Africa from Independence to the Present Day - Read African Books, accessed March 20, 2025, https://www.readafricanbooks.com/opinion/publishing-in-africa-from-independence-to-the-present-day/

65 Coming of Age. Strides in African Publishing, accessed March 20, 2025, https://www.readafricanbooks.com/reviews/coming-of-age/

66 Publishing in Africa from Independence to the Present Day - Read African Books, accessed March 20, 2025, https://www.readafricanbooks.com/opinion/publishing-in-africa-from-independence-to-the-present-day/

67 Publishing in Africa from Independence to the Present Day - Read African Books, accessed March 20, 2025, https://www.readafricanbooks.com/opinion/publishing-in-africa-from-independence-to-the-present-day/

68 African publishing is being revolutionised – report explores trends in 6 countries, accessed March 20, 2025, https://www.bizcommunity.com/article/african-publishing-is-being-revolutionised-report-explores-trends-in-6-countries-144136a

69 Study on the Publishing Landscapes in Sub-Saharan Africa, accessed March 20, 2025,

African publishers south of the Sahara directly impede their capacity to invest in marketing, distribution, and the publication of literature beyond mainstream educational materials. The need for survival often necessitates a focus on more commercially viable textbook publishing, leaving less scope for promoting culturally significant but potentially less profitable works. The increasing use of crowdfunding and grants reflects the resilience and innovation within the African publishing community but also underscores the systemic lack of robust financial support within the local ecosystem. The historical context of colonial influence and subsequent economic structural adjustment policies has had a lasting detrimental effect on the development of a strong and independent African publishing industry, placing local publishers at a significant disadvantage compared to better-resourced multinational corporations.

Multinational corporations exert significant control over South Africa's publishing sector. They hold a substantial 60% of educational publishing, which comprises 80% of the country's entire publishing industry. This leaves a smaller portion of the total publishing market for local publishers. White-owned companies control 12% of the total market, while black-owned companies have a much smaller share, at 4%. This data highlights the strong multinational presence and the challenges faced by local, particularly black-owned, publishers within the South African publishing landscape.

Several factors are substantiated by the evidence: textbook publishing dominates the African publishing landscape, multinational corporations hold significant control over the South African market (particularly in educational publishing, which is a large portion of the industry), and publishing remains largely inaccessible to

---

https://internationalpublishers.org/study-on-the-publishing-landscapes-in-sub-saharan-africa/

the majority of Africans. While multinational content has, in a historical context, undervalued African creativity, the present situation is more complex. There are increasing efforts by local publishers to counter this, and African artistic expression is gaining greater global recognition. Nevertheless, African publishers face numerous challenges, notably a lack of resources, that hinder their growth and their ability to promote diverse literary works.

Conclusion

Henry Chakava's legacy stands as a monumental testament to the power of vision and unwavering dedication in shaping the African literary landscape. His pioneering work in indigenous publishing in Kenya, and indeed across Africa, transcends mere achievement; it represents a profound cultural transformation. His influence extended globally, notably through his role as a visiting lecturer at Oxford Brookes University, where he earned an honorary doctorate in 2005(Kamau 2016:12)[70], significantly contributing to the international discourse on African literature and publishing.

Chakava's commitment to African languages, his significant contributions to translation, and his resolute challenge to multinational dominance redefined the Kenyan literary scene. His pivotal role as a founding member of the African Books Collective (ABC) underscored his understanding of the critical importance of collaboration and international reach for African voices. He championed inclusivity, ensuring African literature would not only survive but flourish, reaching new heights.

---

[70] A Giant of African Publishing has Fallen - Africa Speaks, accessed March 12, 2025, https://africaspeaks.global/a-giant-of-african-publishing-has-fallen/

However, this journey was not without formidable obstacles. Chakava navigated a publishing landscape often dominated by profit-driven textbook production, where the nuanced voices of African fiction and alternative perspectives struggled to be heard. He lamented the lack of editorial support, highlighting the need for patient guidance in nurturing African writers. He confronted the cyclical volatility of the African publishing sector, the challenges of weakly structured organisations, and the persistent issues of content quality, technical proficiency, and effective distribution.

Moreover, he faced the overwhelming dominance of multinational corporations, striving to carve out space for authentic African creativity and cultural content. These challenges, coupled with the ever-present spectre of censorship and financial constraints, underscored the magnitude of his accomplishments.

Despite these persistent hurdles, Chakava's vision of a vibrant and independent African publishing ecosystem remains a guiding force in the digital age. As Walter Bgoya notes, the landscape has shifted dramatically since 1984, when Chakava proposed "a minimum capital sum of US $250,000" to establish "An Autonomous African Publishing House." Bgoya observes, "With innovations in manuscript preparation and printing such as print-on-demand, one can start with much less than that. What we are presently seeing is the mushrooming of small publishers and self-publishers who are fostering marginalised fields of knowledge including local language publishing, poetry, and autobiographies." [71]

Chakava's profound impact on the accessibility and diversity of literature in Kenya and beyond is undeniable. His story powerfully reminds us of the

---

[71] Walter Bgoya, "Henry Chakava (1946 – 2024): The publisher who pricked the people into consciousness", https://africanarguments.org/2024/04/henry-chakava-the-publisher-who-pricked-the-people-into-consciousness/, accessed March 19, 2025.

transformative potential of individual dedication in shaping cultural identity and intellectual discourse.

As we look to the future, it is crucial to build upon Chakava's legacy. This includes investing in infrastructure and training to enhance the capacity of local publishers through improved access to funding, technology, and skills development. It also involves promoting multilingualism by supporting the publication and dissemination of works in African languages to foster cultural pride and broaden readership. Strengthening networks is another vital aspect, facilitating collaboration among African publishers, writers, and other stakeholders to create a more robust and sustainable publishing ecosystem. Finally, it is essential to leverage technology, utilising digital platforms and innovative solutions to improve distribution, reduce costs, and reach new audiences (Jay 2007, 2016:213-215; Stringer 2016; Aina & Mutula 2007; Wafawarowa 2007; Manji 2007).

In an era marked by globalisation and cultural homogenisation, preserving and promoting African literature is more critical than ever. Chakava's work serves as an inspiration to continue this vital mission, ensuring that African voices are heard, celebrated, and valued on the global stage.

Though his presence will be deeply missed, Henry Chakava's legacy will continue to inspire generations of publishers and writers, reinforcing the enduring power of literature to challenge norms, promote social growth, and celebrate the rich tapestry of African voices.

References

Aina, L.O. and Mutula, S. M. (2007) "Opportunities for Electronic Publishing in Africa", in: Alois Mlambo (ed.), *African Scholarly Publishing Essays*, Oxford: African Books Collective Ltd. & Uppsala: Dag Hammarskjöld Foundation. pp.193-200.

Bgoya, W. (2016) "Foreword", in: Kiarie Kamau & Kirimi Mitambo (eds), *Coming of Age: Studies in African Publishing. Essays in Honour of Dr Henry Chakava@70*, East African Educational Publishers: Nairobi, pp. v-xiii.

Chakava, H. (1977) "Publishing in a Multilingual Situation: the Kenya Case", *The African Book Publishing Record*, UNESCO. Pp.83-90.

Chakava, H. (1988) "A Decade of Publishing in Kenya: 1977-1987. One Man's Involvement", *The African Publishing Record*, pp.235-241.

Chakava, H. (1996a) "Publishing Ngugi: The Challenge, the Risk and the Reward", *Matatu*, Vol.15-16(1):183-200. DOI: https://doi.org/10.1163/18757421-90000187.

Chakava, H. (1996b) *Publishing in Africa: One Man's Perspective*. Issue 6 of Bellagio studies in publishing, Bellagio Publishing Network.

Chakava, H. (2007) "Scholarly Publishing in Africa: The Perspective of an East African Commercial and Textbook Publisher", in: Alois Mlambo (ed.), *African Scholarly Publishing Essays*, Oxford: African Books Collective Ltd. & Uppsala: Dag Hammarskjöld Foundation. pp.66-75.

Chakava, H. (2018) "The Turning Point: Ngũgĩ wa Thiong'o & His Kenyan Publisher." In: Simon Gikandi and Ndirangu Wachanga (eds), *Ngũgĩ. Reflections on his Life of Writing*, Woodbridge: James Currey, an imprint of Boydell & Brewer Ltd, pp.115-120.

Chumbow B.S (2005) The language question and national development in Africa. In: Mkandawire T (ed.) *African Intellectuals: Rethinking Politics, Language, Gender and Development*. Dakar: CODESRIA/Zed, 165–192.

Chumbow BS (2009) Linguistic diversity, pluralism and national development in Africa. *Africa Development* 34(2): 21–45.

Currey, J. (2008) *Africa Writes Back: The African Writers Series & the Launch of African Literature*, Oxford: James Currey Ltd.

Currey, J. (2016) "The Triangle that Defined AWS: Nairobi –Ibadan – London", in: Kiarie Kamau & Kirimi Mitambo (eds), *Coming of Age: Studies in African Publishing. Essays in Honour of Dr Henry Chakava@70*, East African Educational Publishers: Nairobi, pp. 27-41.

Devisch R (2002) *Endogenous Knowledge Practices, Cultures and Sciences: Some Anthropological Perspectives.* Unpublished paper.

Devisch R (2007) The university of Kinshasa: From Lovanium to Unikin. In: Afolayan MO (ed.) *Higher Education in Postcolonial Africa: Paradigms of Development, Decline and Dilemmas.* Trenton, NJ: Africa World Press, 17–38.

Fonlon B.N (2012 [1964]) "A Case for Early Bilingualism/Pour un Bilinguisme de bonne heure" in: *The Task of Today and Other Seminal Essays*, Bamenda: Langaa, 193-269.

Fredriksen, B. Brar, S. and Trucano, M. (2015) *Getting Textbooks to Every Child in Sub-Saharan Africa Strategies for Addressing the High Cost and Low Availability Problem*, Washington DC: World Bank.

Gikandi, S. (2016) "Publisher and Intellectual: The Work of Henry Chakava", in: Kiarie Kamau & Kirimi Mitambo (eds), *Coming of Age: Studies in African Publishing. Essays in Honour of Dr Henry Chakava@70*, East African Educational Publishers: Nairobi, pp. 42-56.

Gray, E., Rens, A. and Bruns, K., (2010) *Publishing and Alternative Licensing Models in Africa: Comparative analysis of the South African and Ugandan PALM Studies*, Creative R&D/IDRC: Canada.

Ilieva, E. and Chakava, H. (2016) "East African Publishing and the Academia", in: Kiarie Kamau & Kirimi Mitambo (eds), *Coming of Age: Studies in African Publishing. Essays in Honour of Dr Henry*

Chakava@70, East African Educational Publishers: Nairobi, pp. 106-128.

Jay, M. (2007) "Print on Demand: The ABC Experience", in: Alois Mlambo (ed.), *African Scholarly Publishing Essays*, Oxford: African Books Collective Ltd. & Uppsala: Dag Hammarskjöld Foundation. pp.207-211.

Jay, M. (2016) "Internationalising the African Book", in: Kiarie Kamau & Kirimi Mitambo (eds), *Coming of Age: Studies in African Publishing. Essays in Honour of Dr Henry Chakava@70*, East African Educational Publishers: Nairobi, pp. 201-216.

Jeppie, S. and Diagne, S.B. (eds). (2008). *The Meanings of Timbuktu*, Pretoria: HSRC & CODESRIA.

Kamau, K. (2016) "The Guru of Publishing: Assessing Henry Chakava's Contribution in Africa", in: Kiarie Kamau & Kirimi Mitambo (eds), *Coming of Age: Studies in African Publishing. Essays in Honour of Dr Henry Chakava@70*, East African Educational Publishers: Nairobi, pp. 1-14.

Kamau, K. & Mitambo, K. (eds), (2016) *Coming of Age: Studies in African Publishing. Essays in Honour of Dr Henry Chakava@70*, East African Educational Publishers: Nairobi.

Manji, F. (2007) "Publishing through ICTs for Social Justice in Africa", in: Alois Mlambo (ed.), *African Scholarly Publishing Essays*, Oxford: African Books Collective Ltd. & Uppsala: Dag Hammarskjöld Foundation. pp.212-222.

Mazrui A (1986) *The Africans: A Triple Heritage*. London: BBC.

Mlambo, A. (ed.), (2007) *African Scholarly Publishing Essays*, Oxford: African Books Collective Ltd. & Uppsala: Dag Hammarskjöld Foundation.

Mŭgo, M. G. (2016) "African Orature: Back to the Roots", in: Kiarie Kamau & Kirimi Mitambo (eds), *Coming of Age: Studies in African Publishing. Essays in Honour of Dr Henry Chakava@70*, East African Educational Publishers: Nairobi, pp. 57-69.

Ndi, W. (2008) Venuti, L. (ed.) "The Translation Studies Reader (New York: Routledge, 2004, PP. vii, 541)" Australian Review of Applied Linguistics 31(1):111-114.

Ngũgĩ wa Thiong'o (1986) *Decolonising the Mind: The Politics of Language in African Literature*. London: James Currey.

Ngũgĩ wa Thiong'o (1997) "Detained: A writer's prison diary". In: Grinker RR, Steiner CB (eds) *Perspectives on Africa: A Reader in Culture, History, and Representation*. Oxford: Blackwell, 613–622.

Ngũgĩ wa Thiong'o (2005) "Europhone or African memory: The challenge of the pan-Africanist intellectual in the era of globalisation". In: Mkandawire T (ed.) *African Intellectuals: Rethinking Politics, Language, Gender and Development*. Dakar/London: CODESRIA/Zed, 155–164.

Ngũgĩ wa Thiong'o (2016) "Henry Chakava: The Gory and Glory of African Language Publishing", in: Kiarie Kamau & Kirimi Mitambo (eds), *Coming of Age: Studies in African Publishing. Essays in Honour of Dr Henry Chakava@70*, East African Educational Publishers: Nairobi, pp. 15-26.

Nyamnjoh, F. B. (2004) "A relevant education for African development – some epistemological considerations", *African Development* 23(1): 161–184.

Nyamnjoh, F. B. (2008) "Children, Media and Globalisation: A Research Agenda for Africa" in: Norma Pecora, Enyonam Osei-Hwere & Ulla Carlsson (eds), *Yearbook 2008: African Media, African Children*. The UNESCO International Clearinghouse on Children, Youth and Media: NORDICOM Goteborg University. (pp.29-48).

Nyamnjoh, F. B. (2012) "Potted Plants in Greenhouses: A Critical Reflection on the Resilience of Colonial Education in Africa", *Journal of Asian and African Studies*, 47(2): 129-154.

Nyamnjoh, F. B. (2016) "Shared Visions and Challenges in Publishing Africa: Henry Chakava and

CODESRIA", in: Kiarie Kamau & Kirimi Mitambo (eds), *Coming of Age: Studies in African Publishing. Essays in Honour of Dr Henry Chakava@70*, East African Educational Publishers: Nairobi, pp. 159-186.

Nyamnjoh, F. B. (2017) *Drinking from the Cosmic Gourd: How Amos Tutuola Can Change Our Minds*, Bamenda: Langaa.

Nyamnjoh, F.B., and Shoro, K. (2011) "Language, Mobility, African Writers and Pan-Africanism", *African Communication Research*, 4(1): 35-62.

Nyamnjoh, F. B., Nwosu, P. and Yosimbom, H.M. (eds) (2021) *Being and Becoming African as a Permanent Work in Progress: Inspiration from Chinua Achebe's Proverbs*, Bamenda: Langaa.

Nyariki, L. (2016) "Lobby for the Book: The Politics of African Publishing and the Growth of Professional and Trade Organisations", in: Kiarie Kamau & Kirimi Mitambo (eds), *Coming of Age: Studies in African Publishing. Essays in Honour of Dr Henry Chakava@70*, East African Educational Publishers: Nairobi, pp. 217-235.

Ojeniyi, A. (2016) "The Dominance of the Textbook in African Publishing", in: Kiarie Kamau & Kirimi Mitambo (eds), *Coming of Age: Studies in African Publishing. Essays in Honour of Dr Henry Chakava@70*, East African Educational Publishers: Nairobi, pp. 70-94.

Olukoshi, A. and Nyamnjoh, F. B. (2007) "CODESRIA: Over 30 Years of Scholarly Publishing", in: Alois Mlambo (ed.), *African Scholarly Publishing Essays*, Oxford: African Books Collective Ltd. & Uppsala: Dag Hammarskjöld Foundation. pp.57-65.

Stringer, R. (2016) "African Publishing in the Digital Age", in: Kiarie Kamau & Kirimi Mitambo (eds), *Coming of Age: Studies in African Publishing. Essays in Honour of Dr Henry Chakava@70*, East African Educational Publishers: Nairobi, pp. 187-200.

Venuti, L. ed. (2004) *The Translation Studies Reader.* New York: Routledge.

Wafawarowa, B. (2007) "Digital Print on Demand for African Publishing", in: Alois Mlambo (ed.), *African Scholarly Publishing Essays*, Oxford: African Books Collective Ltd. & Uppsala: Dag Hammarskjöld Foundation. pp.201-206.

Zell, H.M., (2008) *Publishing, Books & Reading in Sub-Saharan Africa: A Critical Bibliography*, Hans Zell Publishing, Lochcarron, Wester Ross, Scotland.

Zell, H.M., and Thierry, R. (2015) *Book Donation Programmes for Africa: Time for A Reappraisal? Two Perspectives*, Hans Zell Publishing, Lochcarron, Wester Ross, Scotland.

www.ingramcontent.com/pod-product-compliance
Ingram Content Group UK Ltd.
Pitfield, Milton Keynes, MK11 3LW, UK
UKHW042016190726
13854UKWH00005B/2306